CW01465868

Proofreading Skillz
A Guided Workbook To Help You Improve Your Grammar and Punctuation

by Teline Guerra

Mad Skills Academics
madskillzacademics.com

Copyright © 2017 by Teline Guerra
All rights reserved. This book or any portion thereof
may not be reproduced or used in any manner whatsoever
without the express written permission of the publisher
except for the use of brief quotations in a book review.

First Printing, 2017

Mad Skillz Academics

www.madskillzacademics.com

CONTENTS

YOU are the key to your success. YOU can achieve your goals.

READ THIS FIRST

Hey! Welcome!

Come in. Pull up a seat. Make yourself comfortable. Welcome to class. It's a cool class where you can sit where you want and there are no walls.

Get a good seat. We are going to be together for a while.

You:

You are back in college after some time in the workforce. You are new to college and feeling behind. You want your writing to be cleaner, more professional. You are eager to succeed. You are ready to improve your proofreading skills.

Awesome. First of all, let's give you a round of applause. Many people find writing and grammar intimidating. Some people have been convinced that they simply don't have what it takes to be good at punctuation. Some people are scared.

What you are about to do is an act of courage. Working to better yourself is always an act of courage.

You are here because you need this skill. You have come to learn. I am here to help you.

This will not be easy. I wish we lived in the Matrix and that I could plug this information into your brain and make you an instant grammar Kung Fu expert—or at least give us all black leather trench coats. Unfortunately, in the real world, we have to work for what we want.

Me:

I'm an English professor. I have had thousands of students come through my classes. Some had serious grammar phobia. Some had an issue with one or two things. In college, we don't teach proofreading. We can't. We don't have time.

In a perfect world, you would have mastered proofreading before you get to college. This is not a perfect world. Do you remember diagraming sentences in elementary school? You did that in order to learn punctuation. Unfortunately, many schools fail, or if you have been away from school for a while, it is very easy to forget what you once knew.

There is no shame in being where you are, and you are not alone. Take control of your life. Learn all the tools you need to succeed.

Time and time again, I have had students come to me and ask

READ THIS FIRST

how they could get better at proofreading. I have told them to watch YouTube videos and look at ESL websites. But I knew these were not what they needed.

So I made this.

This:

This is book, along with the videos and the website, are exactly what I do with my students to get them up to speed on proofreading. These are the things I have done; these are the things that have worked.

First, I explain how grammar, punctuation, and sentences work. Some of what I am explaining is going to seem too basic for you. Great! Those sections are a reminder of what you already know.

Each new topic builds on the learning from the chapters before. So follow the book in order.

Second, I give you exercises. Grammar and punctuation are skills, and skills come from practice. Unlike the Matrix, a real King Fu expert has done the same move a thousand times.

Does it seem repetitive? Great! Repeating things takes them from things you have to think about to things you do automatically. The best possible way to approach proofreading is to have most of it be automatic.

This book has practice. Lots of practice.

Each chapter ends with practice. Practicing once is not going to make this stick, so the practice is split into seven sections. If you do that practice every day for a week, you will have a much better chance of remembering.

The reason most grammar books fail is that they don't give you useful exercises. They say, "Choose between are and were at this exact point of the sentence." That isn't a real-world skill. Writing is not multiple choice.

When you write, you apply a dozen rules at the same time, and any word could be wrong. So these exercises are, whenever possible, real sentences with real mistakes in them that you can find with your real brain.

You aren't choosing the right answer. You are proofreading. That's the skill we ultimately want you to have, so that is what we will practice.

The other thing about the practice here is that it covers EVERYTHING YOU HAVE LEARNED UP TO THAT POINT. Instead of focusing on one rule for a little while and then setting it

The skill you need is the ability to spot a mistake in a sentence when you don't have a hint about what the mistake could be.

Go to madskillzacademics.com for videos and support as you go through the lessons.

READ THIS FIRST

aside to focus on another rule, the exercises in this book build. By the end of the book, you will be practicing everything you learned.

The answers to the practice questions are here for you so that you can check your progress. If you need more in-depth explanations of the answers, go to madskillzacademics.com where you can ask questions and get clarification.

Third, test your skills. At the end of the book, you will find grammar tests. These are short essays, each with fifty mistakes. Find the fifty mistakes and correct them. If you can do that, you have this mastered.

Not there yet? Go back. Review more. Practice more. Try again.

You will be as successful as the effort you put in. I am not there with you to look over your shoulder and force you to work. You are in college. Your college success is in your hands. You have to motivate yourself to do this work.

There is one other thing you need to understand about this book. It is not comprehensive. People spend their whole lives studying English grammar. It's a complicated language. If you decide after this course that you want to delve deeper, awesome! Great! That's terrific!

But this book is about getting everyone a working knowledge that will help you write clean academic essays and someday, appropriate business documents. Our goal is to achieved the level of skill all college graduates ought to have, regardless of major.

If you put in the time, I promise you will improve.

Proofreading is not the same as writing, and it isn't something you should do while you are writing. It's something you should do after you are done writing, as a separate step in your writing process.

Trying to write and proofread at the same time is like trying to juggle and play a trumpet at the same time. They are processes that impede one another. You will make your first big strides in your writing when you do these two things separately.

When we proofread, we are looking for errors in grammar and punctuation.

But what is grammar anyhow? Grammar is the rules of a language. They evolve over time and are key to making words meaningful. Without grammar, we'd speak in lists, and we would have a terrible time expressing anything even slightly complex.

If you are a native speaker of English, great news! You've been learning English grammar since you were born. If you learned English as a second language, you know how lucky those native English speakers are. English is one of the more difficult languages to

---

Proofreading is NOT writing! These are two different mental functions and if you try to do them at the same time, you will do both of them poorly. **Write.** When you finish writing, then proofread. Always proofread as a separate step.

READ THIS FIRST

learn because English is essentially three languages crushed together into one.

This book does not cover ESL issues. There are many other excellent guides to help you if you are an ESL student.

Proofreading for grammar should mostly involve looking for errors that would sound wrong if you said them aloud. If you were raised in a family that didn't speak Standard English, you might have more difficulty with some grammar rules. You may have to approach some parts of grammar as though English is your second language. While this may cause you difficulties, remember that there really isn't a "better" or "worse" version of any language. It's more like clothing. Overalls and boots are appropriate for a lot of situations, but if you want to fit in at formal dinner, you have to get yourself the right clothes.

Any language that does the job of a language—expresses meaningful messages that can be understood by others—is a good language.

Proofreading for punctuation is different. While grammar is an essential part of language and is developed by the speakers of that language over centuries, punctuation was invented by people to help written communication make sense.

Take any paragraph that you've read so far and imagine it without the periods and commas. It would be a nightmare to read. Good punctuation is there to make writing clear. That clarity comes when punctuation fits grammar. This is why we have to understand grammar to proofread well.

The dirty little secret of punctuation is that the rules change over time. Some things go in and out of fashion. Several punctuation marks all do the same job. Some you will never need to use. Wherever possible in this book, I have ignored the nuances of punctuation to give you clear, easy to follow rules. I will tell you when I do that. Remember, our goal that you develop your proofreading skills to a college level. We are learning to ride the bike from point A to point B. Once you get this down, you can learn to do cool tricks, like wheelies. Are the kids still doing wheelies?

You get the point.

Here are the tools you need. Now it's up to you to improve your proofreading skills

STEP ONE: Understand
STEP TWO: Practice

If someone ever told you to put commas where you pause in the sentence, let's take a moment to shake our fists.

A lazy teacher misled you. Commas are not about pauses. They are about grammar.

PARTS OF SPEECH

Let's start at the very beginning. The most fundamental unit of grammar is words, and words fall into different categories called parts of speech.

In a sentence, every word is doing a job. Some words can do lots of different jobs, some can only do one. That job could be noun or verb or conjunction.

You could try to memorize what every single word can do-- and if you learned English as a second language, then you did some of that--but for those of us who are native speakers of English, it will be easier to learn the jobs and learn how to recognize what role a word is playing.

You might think this section is too basic, but go over it anyhow. Refresh your memory.

Nouns

NOUNS:
a person, place, thing or idea

A noun is a person, place, or thing. If you can touch it, it is definitely a noun. Ted is a noun. Chocolate cake is a noun. Nebraska is a noun. But nouns can also be abstract ideas. Liberty is a noun. Freedom is a noun.

There are sub-categories of nouns like pronouns and proper nouns. We will look at these more closely later, but they are still doing the work of nouns.

Verbs

VERBS:
action words or state of being

Verbs are action words. Verbs are also words that indicate state of being. That, however, is far simpler than it sounds, because in English, only one verb indicates state of being: to be. You may recognize to be in its other forms: is, was, am, were, been.

In a verb's most basic form, we put the word "to" in front of it. We call this the infinitive form. To eat, to cry, to dance, to sing, to swim, to write, to sit.

When you see a verb that has the word "to" in front of it, you can treat the whole thing as a unit.

The way verbs change-- to eat becomes ate or eaten--is a key feature of how sentences are built. When a verb changes its form like that, we call it conjugating.

PARTS OF SPEECH
Modifiers

You probably learned this category as adverbs and adjectives. That is still a true division, but we are learning parts of speech in order to proofread, and for the sake of proofreading, I prefer to lump them all together.

Modifiers are words that tell us more information about nouns and verbs and sometimes other modifiers.

Cat is a noun. Fat cat tells us more about the cat. Fat modifies the word cat.

MODIFIERS:
words that give more information about another word

(adjectives and adverbs)

Articles

Here's an easy one. There are only three articles in English, and these three words are only ever articles.

They are a, an, and the.

Got it? All the articles in English:

a, an, the

Articles mark nouns. They tell us if a noun is meant generally or specifically.

If I ask for a pencil, then any pencil will do.

If I ask for the pencil, then there is only one pencil I want.

ARTICLES:
a, an ,the

Conjunctions

Conjunctions are linking words. They do the job of attaching words, phrases, and clauses together, and tell us the relationship of the link as they do so.

Every single way we know how to group words, conjunctions do the connecting.

There are four different subcategories of conjunctions. Two are very important, and you use them constantly. We will start with those.

CONJUNCTIONS:
words that link together words, phrases, and clauses

Coordinating Conjunctions

These conjunctions link equal elements together. There's a mnemonic device for remembering coordinating conjunctions; you may have heard it before.

FANBOYS
For And Nor But Or Yet So

Coordinating conjunctions
FANBOYS:
For, And, Nor, But, Or, Yet, So

PARTS OF SPEECH

This is a complete list of coordinating conjunctions in English. But watch out. "For" can also be a preposition. "So that" is a subordinating conjuction. You have to see how the word is used.

To link words:
 peas and carrots
to link phrases
to be or not to be
to link clauses:
I went to the store, so you can get your butt up off the couch.

Subordinating Conjunctions

These conjunctions link clauses together, and they indicate that one clause is dependent on the other clause. We will definitely talk more about this later.

There is no easy way to remember these kinds of conjunctions; the list of words that fit in this category is much longer. But if you understand how these words work, it will be easy to spot when a word is doing this job.

What I do is I learned to spot words that were joining clauses together, and if it isn't a coordinating conjunction, it is probably a subordinating conjunction. We will be discussing clauses in the future. You need to find your own way to remember these very important words.

Correlative Conjunctions

We can use two words to link things instead of one.
Either good or bad
Neither up nor down
If you treat these situations the same way you treat coordinating conjunctions, you will punctuate them correctly.

Conjunctive Adverbs

You may have heard these called transition words.

It is important to be able to spot these, and people often confuse them with subordinating conjunctions. They are punctuated very differently than subordinating conjunctions are, so it's worth it to familiarize yourself with these.

I remember them because they don't really show a strong relationship. Let me show you.
If I have this sentence:

I will give you ten dollars if you pick up your room.

Subordintating Conjunctions

after, although, as, as if, because, before, even though, if, in order that, since, so that, than, that, though,unless, until, when, where, wherever, which, while, who, whom, whose, why

Conjunctive Adverbs

accordingly, also, besides, comparatively, certainly, anyway, in addition, instead, namely, next, indeed, however, meanwhile, moreover, therefore, thus
this is not a complete list!

PARTS OF SPEECH

"If" is the subordinating conjunction, and it is showing a strong, specific relationship between the first part, "I will give you ten dollars," and the second part, "you pick up your room."
But if I change it to a conjunctive adverb,

I will give you ten dollars; also, you pick up your room.

Now they aren't cause and effect anymore. The relationship is weaker. That helps me spot the difference. The important thing is that you can tell these two kinds of conjunctions apart, not how you do it. If you refer to the dictionary every time you are uncertain, that is even better.

Prepositions

This is a category of word that is trick to explain. Sometimes people will call them "little words" because so many prepositions are two or three letters long, but some are longer. Prepositions connect nouns or pronouns to the rest of the sentence in a way that adds information.
I found it much more useful to think that prepositions are what you can be to a cloud.

IN a cloud
ON a cloud
INSIDE a cloud (see! not a little word!)
AROUND a cloud
OVER a cloud

Prepositions are important because they make prepositional phrases. That is when a preposition is followed by a noun. All of these examples are prepositional phrases, which then work as a special kind of modifier.

Interjections

This category of words is my favorite.
Interjections are words that don't really have meaning. They express emotion. That's it. Emotion. This is the category of word where you can make something up, and it is still a word. In the movie *The 40-Year-Old Virgin*, there's a scene where Steve Carrel is getting his chest waxed, and he yells out "Kelly Clarkson!" That's an interjection. It doesn't matter what "Kelly Clarkson" usually means. He is using it to express extreme emotion, pain.

Prepositions

about, above, across, after, against, along, among, around, as, at, before, behind, below, beside, between, beyond, by, down, during, except, for, from, in, inside, into, like, near, of, off, on, onto, out, over, past, round, since, through, to, toward, under, up, upon, with, within, without
this is not a complete list!

Interjections!

Anything that you say to express emotion is an interjection.
Wah! Duh! Gulp!

11

PARTS OF SPEECH

These are words like "wow," "aw," or "d'oh!" Swear words often fit in this category.

To punctuate interjections, you can either attach them to a sentence with a comma, or you can give them an exclamation point of their own. These will look like fragments but are acceptable.

Aw, flip, I've finished talking about interjections. Boo.

So those are the parts of speech. Seven categories of words. Seven different jobs a word can do in a sentence. But words can do multiple jobs.

Take the word "chair." That' a noun. It's a thing that I can touch and sit on, but it can also be used as a verb:

Sarah will chair the committee.

If you assume chair is always a noun and you don't look at the job it is doing in the sentence, you will have problems.

Words can change the part of speech that they are able to do over time. Take the word google. For a good long time, google meant nothing. It was like goo goo or ffftttt. It was just nonsense sounds represented by letters.

However, one day, a mathematician showed his young daughter a one with a million zeros after it, and he asked his daughter to name it. She called it a google, and thus, google began its life as a number. A number can do two jobs. It can be a modifier:

I'd like a google chicken nuggets.

It can also be a noun:

How many chicken nuggets would you like?
I want a google.

Then, a certain tech company took google from the number and used it as its name. Google became a noun in its own right. It became a website, which is a thing, or if you want to get fancy, it's a place on the internet.

So Google the company grew, and eventually, people started to use the word google to mean "to search for something on the internet, probably by using Google's search engine."

I googled myself last night.

Want more on this? Go to madskillzacademics.com.

12

PARTS OF SPEECH

If you don't know when the movie starts, google it. And google became a verb.

Words. They are fun.

THAT

Before we move on to the practice, I want to talk for a moment about one particular word. No other word in English acts like this word.

"That" can do a whole bunch of jobs. It can be a noun, a modifier, or a conjunction. Many words do more than one job. What makes "that" special is that is can disappear.

That's right. Disappear. It's still there, doing its job, but you can't see it. This word is a ninja.

It only does this when it is being a subordinating conjunction. Here's an example:

I worry John won't make it.

Do you see it? The invisible that?

I worry THAT John won't make it.

The good news is that when you have an invisible that, you don't need a comma. The bad news is that while you are just starting out learning about grammar and punctuation, you are very likely to be tricked a few times by the invisible that.

Don't worry. After it tricks you a few times, you'll learn to watch out for the invisible that.

THAT
It can disapear but still be there. It's a ninja.
Pay attention or it will get you!

PARTS OF SPEECH

Parts of Speech
EXERCISES

REMEMBER:
Do one section and then rest. Don't do everything at once.

nouns- person, place, thing, or abstract concept
verbs- action or state of being
modifier- tells us more about another word
article- a , an, the
preposition- what you can do to a cloud
conjunction- linking word
interjection- shows emotion

Label the part of speech of each word in the following sentences.

ONE

1. Over the river and through the woods, to grandmother's house we go.

2. I want the opportunity to be in a class where my classmates are all excellent and admirable, and the teacher is teaching to that level.

3. They are facing the abyss and they know it.

4. Crap, John, we missed the last train to Frankfurter!

5. You wear armor so that nothing will touch you.

6. I can't get enough.

7. In the event of an accident, your seat cushion can be used as a floatation device.

8. But those with the courage to go forward discover that there is something more.

9. Carol Burnett seemed to be having so much fun, and she gave the audience so much joy.

10. When she was the cleaning lady, she'd stop and lean on her mop.

TWO

1. In total, I have seven years of experience in karate, taking classes and fighting.

2. There was a rapt silence as the audience waited to see what she would do.

PARTS OF SPEECH

3. Getting from place to place can be difficult when a person has lost access to a car.

4. When do we have to get the diamond back to the enchanted temple to break the spell?

5. As the preacher speaks, Sarah grips Henry's hand one last time and bends over to kiss his forehead.

6. Sitting on the dock of the bay, I'm watching the tide roll away.

7. You can't handle the truth!

8. I have a dream that my four little children will one day live in a nation where they will not be judged by the color of their skin but by the content of their character.

9. However, Jose preferred the offer that Yale made to him: a full-ride scholarship and a lifetime supply of oatmeal cream pies.

10. Say "hello" to my little friend!

THREE

1. Today, I consider myself the luckiest man on the face of the earth.

2. Trappist Monk Thomas Merton wrote in his book, Contemplative Prayer, "I cannot discover my 'meaning' if I try to evade the dread which comes from first experiencing my meaninglessness!"

3. Oh, say, can you see by the dawn's early light what so proudly we hailed at the twilight's last gleaming?

4. In order to survive a zombie apocalypse, a resourceful person needs to be willing to sacrifice any friend or family member.

5. We are not here on this earth to pass through undamaged.

6. Hey! Watch out!

Parts of Speech
EXERCISES

Remember: contractions are two words blended together, and they are usually NOT the same part of speech. "I'm" is "I am," a noun and a verb.

Parts of Speech
EXERCISES

Having trouble telling how a word is being used?

Remember: the dictionary lists every part of speech that a word can be used, and examples.

Look up words at merriam-webster.com

7. I'm mad as hell, and I'm not going to take it anymore!

8. You can see it when a team runs out on the field, whooping and dancing with slightly strained smiles.

9. Damn, Daniel!

10. Curse these shackles that you put on me.

FOUR

1. We hold these truths to be self-evident, that all men are created equal, that they are endowed by their creator with certain unalienable Rights, that among these are Life, Liberty, and the pursuit of Happiness.

2. Oh my gosh, this tank top is only ten bucks!

3. The undersigned, known forthwith as the renter, agrees to the terms set forth by the landlord in this contract.

4. Someday, I hope to shake Martha Stewart's hand and thank her for all the amazing cookie recipes.

5. Toto, I've a feeling we're not in Kansas anymore.

6. I know that this is a controversial stance, but I prefer oatmeal raisin cookies to chocolate chip, especially in situations where I don't know the baker of the cookies.

7. You decided to dip, but now you want to trip cause another brother noticed me.

8. The newest version of the highway allows for more traffic; however, the benefits of the increase in traffic are offset by the cost of the project.

9. Do you need more high speed data?

10. Baby, if I knew what it was, I wouldn't have called it a "weird sparking thing."

FIVE

1. In 1969, Celestial Seasonings began picking fresh herbs in the forests and canyons of the Rocky Mountains and blending them to create healthy, flavorful teas.

2. While fruit bearing trees are far more numerous, pine trees are older, having been growing when dinosaurs roamed the earth.

3. The greatest difficulty in fighting zombies is overcoming the natural desire not to hurt another human being, but you must remember that zombies are no longer human.

4. Nobody will ever deprive the American people of the right to vote except the American people themselves, and the only way they could do this is by not voting.

5. It smells like burnt baloney and regrets down here.

6. One very good reason that dogs are better than cats is that dogs actually do things that need to be done, like bomb sniffing and barking at strangers.

7. Hey! Now we've got problems, and I don't think we can solve them.

8. You can always count on Americans to do the right thing -- after they've tried everything else.

9. The first dogs were canids that lingered near human encampment, eating the trash that people even back then produced in large quantities.

10. One issue with the counseling department is that they are hard to get ahold of.

Parts of Speech
EXERCISES

Studies have shown that taking a break between educational exercises increases long term retention. You learn better when you space out your practice.

Parts of Speech
EXERCISES

The word "will" can be a noun when you mean determination: Where there's a will, there's a way.

And it can be part of the conjugation of a verb that means that the thing happens in the future:
I will survive!

In this case, call it a verb. It is not an action word, but it is essential to the verb.

SIX

1. And for the support of this Declaration, with a firm reliance on the protection of Divine Providence, we mutually pledge to each other out Lives, our Fortunes, and our sacred Honor.

2. Once it was my turn, I typed in the name of my topic and waited for the computer to give me the information.

3. While I enjoy the portability of the iPad, it doesn't do enough real work to be useful in an office setting.

4. Ma'am, can you tell us where you got the world's tiniest bow tie?

5. If you are not delighted, we will make it right with a replacement or refund at your store.

6. To sum up, because the sink in question drains to pipes shared by multiple apartments, it is impossible to state that the tenant is clearly responsible.

7. Boy, am I sick of writing sentences.

8. Standing in the light of your halo, I got my angel now.

9. The average wait time to see a counselor has been three weeks, every semester.

10. The first settlers in New England were very aware of the effects of religious persecution because they had experienced it in England, but they still made laws dictating what people could believe.

SEVEN

1. Never compare me to the mayor in Jaws! Never!

2. There are a lot of ways to get killed, and she seems to stumble into every single one.

PARTS OF SPEECH

3. He informed me that it was because the other sinks involved were likely above mine, and that due to gravity, my sink would back up while the higher sink would not.

4. When I am eating a new cookie, I am always paying attention to the level of sweetness and flavor and also to the cookie's softness.

5. In order to make a cheesy ham and potato casserole, you will need to gather together one onion, a package of frozen hash browns, one can of cream of chicken soup, and diced ham.

6. The best place to get donuts in Portland is Blue Ribbon donuts, but you need to get there before they run out.

7. Okay, okay, ladies, now let's get in formation cause I slay.

8. In the restaurant, a grizzled old man with no teeth and a jaded young detective sat discussing the murder case and the apple pie.

9. Sonia felt terrible about it, but she had to hire someone to help her clean before she went completely insane.

10. If I were planning my last meal on earth, I would have fillet mignon, mashed potatoes, and eight different kinds of donuts.

Parts of Speech
EXERCISES

REMEMBER:
Our goal is to get better. Our goal is not perfection. So if this comes slowly, give yourself a break. Learning slowly is still learning.

The answers to these exercises are in the back of this book.

GERUNDS

3

When a verb ends in -ing, it can either do the work of a verb or it can do the work of a noun (or other things we will cover later).
How can you tell?

If it's doing the work of a verb, it will have helping verbs in front of it.

I am going to the store.

If it's doing the work of a noun, it won't have a helping verb, and it will relate to the words around it the way a noun would.

Going to the store is my favorite.

Ok, let's throw in a little bit of a monkey wrench.

There is a way in which verbs become nouns. It is called a gerund, and it is made with the -ing ending.

It would be great if we could just spot -ing and know that we have a noun, but that isn't how it works. Sometimes the -ing ending is a verb, sometimes it is a noun. How can you tell the difference?

As a verb, the -ing ending form can't work alone. It has to have other verbs with it. Usually, we are talking about to be verbs.

I am killing zombies.

In this case, "am" is a form of "to be", making killing a verb.

I am tired of killing zombies.

This time, the "to be" goes with tired, not killing. In fact, the word in front of killing is "of," a preposition. And prepositions are followed by nouns or pronouns when they are making prepositional phrases.

So the "of" is another indicator that here, we are talking about a gerund. Killing is doing the job of a noun.

Now, gerunds can stand alone:

Eating is my favorite Olympic sport.

or they can have other words with them:

Eating pizza and donuts is my favorite Olympic sport.

When a gerund has these other words with it, we call that a gerund phrase. "Eating pizza and donuts" is a gerund phrase. The whole phrase is functioning all together as one noun.

But I could have this sentence:

Eating donuts and pizza, I gained forty pounds.

It is the same gerund phrase, but now it isn't doing the work of a noun. It is an introductory element. We haven't covered those yet, but this is another important use of gerunds.

You will see in the next chapter why gerunds are important. For now, let's practice what we have learned.

GERUNDS

ONE

1. Breaking up is hard to do.

2. When I am getting sick, I drink extra orange juice and eat pickles.

3. Lifting over a thousand pounds of steel beams, Superman saved three children and a puppy.

4. Superman was getting a lot of attention for his feats, so he decided to take a Hawaiian vacation.

5. Flying to Hawaii for vacation is easier when you have super powers and don't have to book anything.

TWO

1. Susan likes getting presents for her birthday.

2. However, when her daughter was turning sixteen, Susan tried to pretend that throwing a party was a present.

3. Everyone knows that putting together a party is a lot of work, but she still should have bought a present, even if it was something small.

4. Susan is telling people that her daughter didn't want a present; she wanted a bigger party.

5. This is why judging people without all of the facts can be the wrong thing to do.

THREE

1. Were you watching the news last night?

2. The top story was discussing problems in the Middle East.

3. People are worrying about the children caught in the middle of these conflicts.

4. Questioning our involvement in the Middle East is more important during an election year.

Find the verbs that end in -ing.

Is there a helping verb?
Then it is a verb.
Is there not a helping verb?
Gerund.

Want more on this? Go to madskillzacademics.com.

Gerund
EXERCISES

5. Electing people who represent out values, Americans are able to influence the foreign policy on such issues.

FOUR

1. Working for the man, just trying to make a living, Maria saved up enough money to buy a house in cash.

2. When playing Monopoly, getting out of jail becomes an important goal.

3. It doesn't look good for her; she was caught while fleeing the scene of the crime, covered in glitter.

4. Sitting across from me is my guest this evening, the Honorable Judge Andrea Perkins.

5. Layla dove across the room, hitting the air lock button just as the alien's tentacles wrapped around Arman's neck.

FIVE

1. Arthur knelt by the pond as the Lady in the Lake raised up the sword Excalibur; receiving the sword made Arthur the King of England.

2. In our government system, getting a knife tossed to you by a homeless lady doesn't make you king.

3. In the previous sentence, I was paraphrasing a very funny bit from *Monty Python and The Search for the Holy Grail.*

4. People are opening themselves to new ideas when they watch Monty Python.

5. Saying that Monty Python is as great as Shakespeare, I prove that I am cool and subversive.

GERUNDS

SIX

1. I like ice cream, but John likes getting punched in the face by clowns.

2. Saving frequently prevents people from losing their work in case their computer crashes.

3. Examining the grammar in song lyrics can often be frustrating if a person likes things to be grammatically correct.

4. In my dreams, winning the lottery allows me to live on a sailboat filled with horses.

5. However, the horses are showing their displeasure by jumping off and swimming away.

SEVEN

1. Proofreading seems like it involves learning a lot of crazy rules that don't apply to real life.

2. These crazy rules are rules that you are already following, even if you aren't aware of it.

3. If you ran around saying whatever you wanted to without any rules, no one would understand you.

4. Adults have more difficult learning because the brain becomes less pliable and adults have other things to do.

5. Children spend most of their time chewing on their own feet, so they have plenty of time to learn.

The answers to these exercises are in the back of this book.

CLAUSES

Ok, now that we know the jobs that the words are doing in the sentence, we can start looking for the structure. And that brings us to clauses. Clauses are the building blocks of sentences.

Clauses are a hugely important part of grammar and punctuation. If you understand clauses, then all the rest of the grammar and punctuation rules we discuss will fall easily in to place. It is such an important concept that I urge you not to move on to anything else until you have mastered this.

So what is a clause?

Well, when a noun meets a verb and they fall in love, they form a very special relationship. In fact, the verb will show us that it is in this relationship by transforming to fit the noun. And once they are in this relationship, we will call them a subject and a predicate.

So if I take a perfectly good noun:

Rosa

Noun + verb

and a perfectly good verb:

to eat

verb changes to fit the noun

and put them together:

Rosa ate.

subject and predicate=

I have a clause. Rosa is the subject. Ate is the predicate. Clause. Lovely. Right? And easy.

clause!

So remember: all subjects are nouns. But not all nouns are subjects. All predicates are verbs. But not all verbs are predicates. That's important stuff there. Read it again.

I can take any noun

Liberty, cat, stool, Mom, powdered sugar

and any verb

to dance, to sing, to work, to break, to listen

All subjects are nouns.
Not all nouns are subjects.

And put them together, and I will get a clause:

The cat danced

All predicates are verbs.
Not all verbs are predicates.

Liberty works

Mom sang

The stool broke

Powdered sugar listens

It might not make perfect sense, but it's a clause. And we are such meaning making machines that even things that don't really make sense become poetic and take on meaning.

It is easy to spot clauses when there are only a few words long,but we usually say much more complicated things, and that is where all those other parts of speech come in. In a longer sentence, it gets harder to spot the subject and predicate because of the modifiers and prepositional phrases. Look at this sentence:

CLAUSES

Early in the morning, the first spring birds with
vicious intent descend upon the park to peck and
hunt up juicy worm for their hatchlings.

If I remove the prepositional phrases and the modifiers, what
is the clause?

Birds descend.

This is the skill we are cultivating. If you can see the jobs the words
are doing, you will learn to see through to the heart of the sentence,
the clause.

CLAUSE TYPES

There are two types of clauses. An independent clause is a
subject and a predicate.

A dependent (or subordinate) clause has a subordinating
conjunction and a subject and a predicate. Do you remember the
types of conjunctions? If not, go back a review them.

That's it. There are two kinds of clauses. There is a sub
category of subordinate clause called an adverbial clause that we are
going to ignore because I rarely see students punctuate adverbial
clauses incorrectly. For the curious, the marker on that kind of clause
is that is doesn't have a subject. For everyone else, learn these two
types of clauses. This is important!

independent clause-subject
and predicate

dependent clause-
subordinating conjunction,
subject, and predicate

UNDERSTOOD YOU

There is one more thing we have to cover, the understood
you. When we are making forceful, commanding statements, like

Get over here!
Stand up for your rights!
Buy today!

we are speaking to "you," but we don't say "you."

So in these commands, we mean "you", and the subject of the
sentence is "you," but we don't say "you" because we all understand
that we mean "you."

Understood you--
we issue commands
without saying "you"
because we all know the
"you" is still there as the
subject of the sentence.

You get over here!   subject you predicate get
You stand up for your rights! subject you, predicate stand
You buy today! subject you, predicate buy

Want more on this? Go to
madskillzacademics.com.

CLAUSES

Find the clauses.

Identify if the clauses are independent or dependent.

ONE

1. Over the river and through the woods, to grandmother's house we go.
2. I want the opportunity to be in a class where my classmates are all excellent and admirable, and the teacher is teaching to that level.
3. They are facing the abyss and they know it.
4. Crap, John, we missed the last train to Frankfurter!
5. You wear armor so that nothing will touch you.
6. I can't get enough.
7. In the event of an accident, your seat cushion can be used as a floatation device.
8. But those with the courage to go forward discover that there is something more.
9. Carol Burnett seemed to be having so much fun, and she gave the audience so much joy.
10. When she was the cleaning lady, she'd stop and lean on her mop.

TWO

1. In total, I have seven years of experience in karate, taking classes and fighting.
2. There was a rapt silence as the audience waited to see what she would do.
3. Getting from place to place can be difficult when a person has lost access to a car.
4. When do we have to get the diamond back to the enchanted temple to break the spell?
5. As the preacher speaks, Sarah grips Henry's hand one last time and bends over to kiss his forehead.
6. Sitting on the dock of the bay, I'm watching the tide roll away.

CLAUSES

7. You can't handle the truth!

8. I have a dream that my four little children will one day live in a nation where they will not be judged by the color of their skin but by the content of their character.

9. However, Jose preferred the offer that Yale made to him: a full-ride scholarship and a lifetime supply of oatmeal cream pies.

10. Say "hello" to my little friend!

THREE

1. Today, I consider myself the luckiest man on the face of the earth.

2. Trappist Monk Thomas Merton wrote in his book, Contemplative Prayer, "I cannot discover my 'meaning' if I try to evade the dread which comes from first experiencing my meaninglessness!"

3. Oh, say, can you see by the dawn's early light what so proudly we hailed at the twilight's last gleaming?

4. In order to survive a zombie apocalypse, a resourceful person needs to be willing to sacrifice any friend or family member.

5. We are not here on this earth to pass through undamaged.

6. Hey! Watch out!

7. I'm mad as hell, and I'm not going to take it anymore!

8. You can see it when a team runs out on the field, whooping and dancing with slightly strained smiles.

9. Damn, Daniel!

10. Curse these shackles that you put on me.

FOUR

1. We hold these truths to be self-evident, that all men are created equal, that they are endowed by their creator with certain unalienable Rights, that among these are Life, Liberty, and the pursuit of

Clauses
EXERCISES

What makes a clause dependent (or subordinate, another name for the same thing)?

a subordinating conjunction

Clauses
EXERCISES

In reality, we grammar types distinguish between the complete subject and the simple subject. The complete subject has all the modifiers attached. The complete predicate includes direct objects and indirect objects. The simple subject and predicate are what we are looking for, the core word or words. As you advance, the complete subject and predicate will become more useful to you, but for what we are covering in this book, simple is the way to go.

Happiness.

2. Oh my gosh, this tank top is only ten bucks!

3. The undersigned, known forthwith as the renter, agrees to the terms set forth by the landlord in this contract.

4. Someday, I hope to shake Martha Stewart's hand and thank her for all the amazing cookie recipes.

5. Toto, I've a feeling we're not in Kansas anymore.

6. I know that this is a controversial stance, but I prefer oatmeal raisin cookies to chocolate chip, especially in situations where I don't know the baker of the cookies.

7. You decided to dip, but now you want to trip cause another brother noticed me.

8. The newest version of the highway allows for more traffic; however, the benefits of the increase in traffic are offset by the cost of the project.

9. Do you need more high speed data?

10. Baby, if I knew what it was, I wouldn't have called it a "weird sparking thing."

FIVE

1. In 1969, Celestial Seasonings began picking fresh herbs in the forests and canyons of the Rocky Mountains and blending them to create healthy, flavorful teas.

2. While fruit bearing trees are far more numerous, pine trees are older, having been growing when dinosaurs roamed the earth.

3. The greatest difficulty in fighting zombies is overcoming the natural desire not to hurt another human being, but you must remember that zombies are no longer human.

4. Nobody will ever deprive the American people of the right to vote

except the American people themselves, and the only way they could do this is by not voting.

5. It smells like burnt baloney and regrets down here.

6. One very good reason that dogs are better than cats is that dogs actually do things that need to be done, like bomb sniffing and barking at strangers.

7. Hey! Now we've got problems, and I don't think we can solve them.

8. You can always count on Americans to do the right thing -- after they've tried everything else.

9. The first dogs were canids that lingered near human encampment, eating the trash that people even back then produced in large quantities.

10. One issue with the counseling department is that they are hard to get ahold of.

SIX

1. And for the support of this Declaration, with a firm reliance on the protection of Divine Providence, we mutually pledge to each other out Lives, our Fortunes, and our sacred Honor.

2. Once it was my turn, I typed in the name of my topic and waited for the computer to give me the information.

3. While I enjoy the portability of the iPad, it doesn't do enough real work to be useful in an office setting.

4. Ma'am, can you tell us where you got the world's tiniest bow tie?

5. If you are not delighted, we will make it right with a replacement or refund at your store.

6. To sum up, because the sink in question drains to pipes shared by multiple apartments, it is impossible to state that the tenant is clearly responsible.

7. Boy, am I sick of writing sentences.

8. Standing in the light of your halo, I got my angel now.

9. The average wait time to see a counselor has been three weeks, every semester.

10. The first settlers in New England were very aware of the effects of religious persecution because they had experienced it in England, but they still made laws dictating what people could believe.

SEVEN

1. Never compare me to the mayor in Jaws! Never!

2. There are a lot of ways to get killed, and she seems to stumble into every single one.

3. He informed me that it was because the other sinks involved were likely above mine, and that due to gravity, my sink would back up while the higher sink would not.

4. When I am eating a new cookie, I am always paying attention to the level of sweetness and flavor and also to the cookie's softness.

5. In order to make a cheesy ham and potato casserole, you will need to gather together one onion, a package of frozen hash browns, one can of cream of chicken soup, and diced ham.

6. The best place to get donuts in Portland is Blue Ribbon donuts, but you need to get there before they run out.

7. Okay, okay, ladies, now let's get in formation cause I slay.

8. In the restaurant, a grizzled old man with no teeth and a jaded young detective sat discussing the murder case and the apple pie.

9. Sonia felt terrible about it, but she had to hire someone to help her clean before she went completely insane.

10. If I were planning my last meal on earth, I would have fillet mignon, mashed potatoes, and eight different kinds of donuts.

The answers to these exercises are in the back of this book.

SENTENCE TYPES

Our two kinds of clauses can be made into four different types of sentences.

A SIMPLE sentence contains one independent clause.
A COMPOUND sentence has two or more independent clauses.
A COMPLEX sentence has one independent clause and one or more dependent clauses.
A COMPOUND/COMPLEX sentence has two or more independent clauses and one or more dependent clauses.

The good news is that when you learn how to identify these sentence types, you will be able to fix some of the most common punctuation errors.

Why? Sentence types are directly connected to comma rules. Here we are, in chapter five, getting real. The following rules, you will want to memorize. In the essays I grade, I'd say 50% of comma mistakes are covered by these rules.

Here we go.

A COMPOUND sentence needs something between those two independent clauses. Most of the time, these two clauses need to be linked by a comma and a coordinating conjunction. Not a comma. Not a coordinating conjunction. BOTH TOGETHER. The clauses can also be linked by a semicolon. When a semicolon is used, do NOT use a coordinating conjunction. The semicolon is already doing the work that the coordinating conjunction would do. It is not needed.

A complex sentence has two big rules, and one less common rule. Rule one, if the subordinating clause happens before the independent clause, THERE WILL ALWAYS BE A COMMA BETWEEN THEM!!! Rule two, if the independent clause happens before the dependent clause, THERE WILL NEVER BE A COMMA BETWEEN THEM!!!

Now, dependent clauses can show up anywhere in the sentence, even in the middle of the independent clause. When that happens, you will put a comma before and after the dependent clause, but sometimes you can put no commas. This doesn't come up as often, so we are going to focus on the other rules for now.

Remember this.
ind, coordinating conjunction ind
dep, ind
ind dep

5

SIMPLE= 1 independent clause

Compound=2 or more independent clauses

Complex=1 independent and 1 or more dependent clauses

Compound/complex= 2 or more independent clauses and 1 or more dependent clauses

Want more on this? Go to madskillzacademics.com.

SENTENCE TYPES

Sentence Types
EXERCISES

Identify the type of sentence for each of these sentences.

PRACTICE ONE

1. Over the river and through the woods, to grandmother's house we go.

2. I want the opportunity to be in a class where my classmates are all excellent and admirable, and the teacher is teaching to that level.

3. They are facing the abyss and they know it.

4. Crap, John, we missed the last train to Frankfurter!

5. You wear armor so that nothing will touch you.

6. I can't get enough.

7. In the event of an accident, your seat cushion can be used as a floatation device.

8. But those with the courage to go forward discover that there is something more.

9. Carol Burnett seemed to be having so much fun, and she gave the audience so much joy.

10. When she was the cleaning lady, she'd stop and lean on her mop.

PRACTICE TWO

1. In total, I have seven years of experience in karate, taking classes and fighting.

2. There was a rapt silence as the audience waited to see what she would do.

3. Getting from place to place can be difficult when a person has lost access to a car.

4. When do we have to get the diamond back to the enchanted temple to break the spell?

5. As the preacher speaks, Sarah grips Henry's hand one last time and bends over to kiss his forehead.

6. Sitting on the dock of the bay, I'm watching the tide roll away.

7. You can't handle the truth!

8. I have a dream that my four little children will one day live in a

nation where they will not be judged by the color of their skin but by the content of their character.

9. However, Jose preferred the offer that Yale made to him: a full-ride scholarship and a lifetime supply of oatmeal cream pies.

10. Say "hello" to my little friend!

PRACTICE THREE

1. Today, I consider myself the luckiest man on the face of the earth.

2. Trappist Monk Thomas Merton wrote in his book, Contemplative Prayer, "I cannot discover my 'meaning' if I try to evade the dread which comes from first experiencing my meaninglessness!"

3. Oh, say, can you see by the dawn's early light what so proudly we hailed at the twilight's last gleaming?

4. In order to survive a zombie apocalypse, a resourceful person needs to be willing to sacrifice any friend or family member.

5. We are not here on this earth to pass through undamaged.

6. Hey! Watch out!

7. I'm mad as hell, and I'm not going to take it anymore!

8. You can see it when a team runs out on the field, whooping and dancing with slightly strained smiles.

9. Damn, Daniel!

10. Curse these shackles that you put on me.

PRACTICE FOUR

1. We hold these truths to be self-evident, that all men are created equal, that they are endowed by their creator with certain unalienable Rights, that among these are Life, Liberty, and the pursuit of Happiness.

2. Oh my gosh, this tank top is only ten bucks!

3. The undersigned, known forthwith as the renter, agrees to the terms set forth by the landlord in this contract.

Sentence Types
EXERCISES

4. Someday, I hope to shake Martha Stewart's hand and thank her for all the amazing cookie recipes.

5. Toto, I've a feeling we're not in Kansas anymore.

6. I know that this is a controversial stance, but I prefer oatmeal raisin cookies to chocolate chip, especially in situations where I don't know the baker of the cookies.

7. You decided to dip, but now you want to trip cause another brother noticed me.

8. The newest version of the highway allows for more traffic; however, the benefits of the increase in traffic are offset by the cost of the project.

9. Do you need more high speed data?

10. Baby, if I knew what it was, I wouldn't have called it a "weird sparking thing."

PRACTICE FIVE

1. In 1969, Celestial Seasonings began picking fresh herbs in the forests and canyons of the Rocky Mountains and blending them to create healthy, flavorful teas.

2. While fruit bearing trees are far more numerous, pine trees are older, having been growing when dinosaurs roamed the earth.

3. The greatest difficulty in fighting zombies is overcoming the natural desire not to hurt another human being, but you must remember that zombies are no longer human.

4. Nobody will ever deprive the American people of the right to vote except the American people themselves, and the only way they could do this is by not voting.

5. It smells like burnt baloney and regrets down here.

6. One very good reason that dogs are better than cats is that dogs actually do things that need to be done, like bomb sniffing and barking at strangers.

SENTENCE TYPES

7. Hey! Now we've got problems, and I don't think we can solve them.

8. You can always count on Americans to do the right thing -- after they've tried everything else.

9. The first dogs were canids that lingered near human encampment, eating the trash that people even back then produced in large quantities.

10. One issue with the counseling department is that they are hard to get ahold of.

PRACTICE SIX

1. And for the support of this Declaration, with a firm reliance on the protection of Divine Providence, we mutually pledge to each other out Lives, our Fortunes, and our sacred Honor.

2. Once it was my turn, I typed in the name of my topic and waited for the computer to give me the information.

3. While I enjoy the portability of the iPad, it doesn't do enough real work to be useful in an office setting.

4. Ma'am, can you tell us where you got the world's tiniest bow tie?

5. If you are not delighted, we will make it right with a replacement or refund at your store.

6. To sum up, because the sink in question drains to pipes shared by multiple apartments, it is impossible to state that the tenant is clearly responsible.

7. Boy, am I sick of writing sentences.

8. Standing in the light of your halo, I got my angel now.

9. The average wait time to see a counselor has been three weeks, every semester.

10. The first settlers in New England were very aware of the effects of religious persecution because they had experienced it in England, but they still made laws dictating what people could believe.

SIMPLE= 1 independent clause

Compound=2 or more independent clauses

Complex=1 independent and 1 or more dependent clauses

Compound/complex= 2 or more independent clauses and 1 or more dependent clauses

Sentence Types
EXERCISES

The answers to these exercises are in the back of this book.

PRACTICE SEVEN

1. Never compare me to the mayor in Jaws! Never!

2. There are a lot of ways to get killed, and she seems to stumble into every single one.

3. He informed me that it was because the other sinks involved were likely above mine, and that due to gravity, my sink would back up while the higher sink would not.

4. When I am eating a new cookie, I am always paying attention to the level of sweetness and flavor and also to the cookie's softness.

5. In order to make a cheesy ham and potato casserole, you will need to gather together one onion, a package of frozen hash browns, one can of cream of chicken soup, and diced ham.

6. The best place to get donuts in Portland is Blue Ribbon donuts, but you need to get there before they run out.

7. Okay, okay, ladies, now let's get in formation cause I slay.

8. In the restaurant, a grizzled old man with no teeth and a jaded young detective sat discussing the murder case and the apple pie.

9. Sonia felt terrible about it, but she had to hire someone to help her clean before she went completely insane.

10. If I were planning my last meal on earth, I would have fillet mignon, mashed potatoes, and eight different kinds of donuts.

COMPOUND SUBJECT AND PREDICATE

Sometimes, people look at the rules about compound sentences, and they think that whenever they see an "and", they should put a comma. Isn't that easier than learning how sentences are constructed? It is easier, and it is wrong.

Coordinating conjunctions are used to link all kinds of things, and the commas work differently when you are not dealing with compound sentences.

A compound subject is when two or more different nouns are doing the same action.

John and Raul eat paste.

Here, both of these nouns, John and Raul, are doing the same verb, eating. A compound predicate is when a noun does two or more verbs.

John eats paste and fights with Raul.

So John, the noun, has two predicates, eats and fights.

You can have a compound subject and a compound predicate in the same sentence:

John and Raul eat paste and fight with each other.

See that there are no commas here? If my compound subject or predicate had three or more elements, I would need commas. I would treat them like a list. But that is not usually what trips people up.

What trips people up is that compound subjects and predicates can have a lot more words. They can have so many words that they LOOK like a compound sentence, but the number of words means nothing. The underlying grammar is key.

The little old Asian woman with two missing teeth in the front of her smile and the tall stranger from Detroit by way of Boston robbed the bank together.

What do I have here? The subjects are woman and stranger, and they are both robbing a bank. It doesn't matter how many words gather around them. A compound subject with two items means no comma.

chapter

6

compound subject--2 or more things all do the same action

compound predicate-- a thing does 2 or more actions

Want more on this? Go to madskillzacademics.com.

Compound Subject and Predicate
EXERCISES

These paragraphs each have five mistakes. The mistakes are violating only the rules we have discussed so far. Find and correct the mistakes.

COMPOUND SUBJECT AND PREDICATE

The following sentences can have compound subjects, compound predicates, or they can be compound sentences. OR they could not be compound in any way! Figure out which they are.

1. The three women in charge of the equities and futures company gave each employee a survey to determine the quickest way to make a profit.
2. Getting on an airplane, small children and the elderly who need assistance are allowed to board first.
3. For those people who are looking to get out of debt, Dave Ramsey or Suze Ormond wrote books to help and have shows where you can ask questions.
4. The first row of seats is reserved for very important people, and the other seats are open to any ticket holder.
5. To unlock more benefits, the player can earn points or pay a fee.

Alright, let's get some real practice in.

1

A nation's values show in, who that nation chooses to celebrate on its currency. Countries choose the images on money based on national history and the people in those countries often get a vote. Canadian currency has pictures of animals, while American currency has political leaders from the past. Because Chileans make heros of their artists Chilean currency has celebrated poets. Americans would find a dollar bill with Mark Twain's face strange, and might reject it as real money. From this, we could say that Canadians value nature, Americans value politics, and Chileans value literature.

2

Getting up in the morning, has been difficult for me. I am a night owl but I do a few different things to help me get an early start on my day. I get up at the same time every day, and always eat breakfast. Routine is important. It also helps, if I start my day with an appointment. When I can my lovely little dog and I will plan a playdate early in the morning.

COMPOUND SUBJECT AND PREDICATE

3

I locked myself out of my house, because I was not paying attention to which keys I picked up. This annoys me, and embarrasses me in front of my neighbors. If I had done what I was supposed to do I wouldn't have to spend money on a locksmith. I gave a spare key to my friends but they live forty five minutes away. I would give a key to my neighbors but trusting them is hard.

4.

Many students take out huge student loans to get a college degree, because of three false beliefs. The first is that it matters where a college degree comes from but this is not true for the vast majority of people. Most jobs require experience, not a brand name degree. The second is that student loans are how college is done, while millions of dollars in scholarships go unclaimed every year. College students should work while they are in school, and should save money before they go to school. Thousands of students are paying their way through college and will start their lives without the burden of student loans. The third falsehood is the scariest. It is the belief that getting a college degree will be so valuable that the student loan won't be a problem. This is laughably untrue. Truck drivers make more money than teachers. Starting a business does not require a degree. Even lawyers and doctors can end up wanting to pursue disciplines that don't pay very well. Choices are ripped away from students with debt so students should do everything they can to avoid it.

5.

A recent court decision in Oregon determined that dogs are sentient beings. This is legally an amazing shift, because pets were legally considered property before. The case in which this became an issue

Don't forget to space out these exercises. You will have better long term retention working at something for short periods of time over many days than you will by working at something for a couple of hours once.

Compound Subject and Predicate
EXERCISES

You may find stylistic errors in these paragraphs. Stylistic errors are when writing is wordy or unfocused. REMEMBER that we are not working on style! We are working on mechanics! Only correct errors in grammar and punctuation, not phrasing.

The answers to these exercises are in the back of this book.

was one in which police encountered a man abusing a dog. The dog communicated to the police that it was hurt and the police then arrested the man. Property legally cannot communicate anything and the owners can do whatever they want with it. The man's lawyers were using the definition of property to argue that the police acted improperly but the court disagreed. Because a sentient being can communicate certain standards of care must be met by the person responsible for it.

6.

Most people believe that zombies are fictional creatures that could never really exist but zombies are a possibility, because scientists have been known in the past to accidentally create powerful forces. Nuclear weapons, and killer bees were invented by people. Most importantly, there is a species of fungus that attacks ants. This fungus invades the ant's brain, and controls the dead ant's body to enter the nest and spread the fungus. That's a zombie. If the fungus evolves to infect humans a zombie outbreak becomes a real possibility.

7.

Archeologists use bat guano to make great discoveries about the past. Guano is a fancy word for bat poop. Bats seek out caves that are inaccessible from the ground and generations of bats will live in that cave. Because bats hang from the ceiling the guano falls to the ground, and piles up undisturbed over the years in layers. Seeds from the fruits the bats ate, and pollens that get caught in the guano show archeologists what plants lived in the area and those plants reveal the climate.

INTRODUCTORY ELEMENTS

Things that come before the first clause of the sentence are called introductory elements. We say "elements" because this can be phrases or words. Basically, we are talking about words or groups of words before the actual clause.

So if the clause is, "the little old lady fell down," then we can use different introductory elements.

> Unfortunately, the little old lady fell down.
> Behind the store, the little old lady fell down.
> Because of the wet floor, the little old lady fell down.
> Learning Judo, the little old lady fell down.
> To be honest, the little old lady fell down.

See how the introductory element is NOT a modifier of the subject of the sentence. "Unfortunately" does not tell us more about the lady. It comments on the whole sentence.

Introductory elements are separated from the sentence by a comma. This is why we care. To simplify a number of rules, I am going to advise you to always separate the introductory element with a comma. When you get the hang of this, you can add in other rules.

When the introductory element is a prepositional phrase, we have the five word rule. That rule states that if the prepositional phrase is five words or more, it has to have a comma. If less than five words, the comma is optional. This is because at around five words, it starts to be potentially confusing. Am I reading a clause yet? Is this still just introducing the sentence? Commas exist to alleviate confusion.

> In the first light of dawn, the army attacked.

> At dawn, the army attacked.
> At dawn the army attacked.

The comma here creates a slightly different emphasis to the sentence, but doesn't change the meaning or make the sentence more or less clear. I like the comma being there. So I would say, simplify your life, and always add the comma. When you get comfortable, you can change it up.

chapter

7

Anything that precedes the complete subject of the first clause (or the subordinating conjunction of the first clause) is an introductory element. There can also be an introductory element on the second part of a compound sentence.

Want more on this? Go to madskillzacademics.com.

Introductory Elements
EXERCISES

There are five errors in each paragraph. Find and correct them. They could be anything we have covered so far.

1.

Every so often people need to clean out their closets. Old clothes that don't fit anymore, and worn out pairs of sneakers gather in the corners. We think that we will wear these old clothes, when we are painting, but we don't often paint things. We don't really need five different painting options and keeping all these things makes it hard to store and find the things we really use. On the other hand giving away clothes that we aren't using is a small way to help others.

2.

Lately several sleep experts have pointed out that Americans are sleeping less, and sleeping worse than they need to function properly. While these experts point at several different factors one that stands out is sleeping with a dog or a cat in the bed. Dogs and cats move around during the night, waking their owners. Even if people don't wake up the disturbance is often enough to reduce the quality of sleep. To function people need to spend several hours in deep sleep and REM sleep, and a wiggly puppy prevents that.

3.

When people use credit cards, studies have shown that they spend more. In one study, a professor waited outside a store. As people came out he asked them how much they had spent. Afterwards, he had them look at their actual receipt. Interestingly enough he found that people who used credit cards could only guess within five or ten dollars, while people who had paid in cash knew how much they had

INTRODUCTORY ELEMENTS

spent within a dollar. This is one of the reasons that credit cards are dangerous. People are more likely to lose track of their spending with a credit card but they are much clearer on their spending, when they use cash.

4.

When a person gets a dog we say that person has adopted a dog. This is a key change in our attitudes towards dogs and cats. They are family. To people living a hundred years ago a dog was a tool. In those days, people would tie unwanted puppies in a sack, and drop them in a river to dispose of them. When a person gets a dog today, that person is making an emotional commitment to that animal. That person is promising to take care of that animal, until the dog's last breath. It's a big responsibility. This is why a person should give a lot of consideration to the commitment involved before acquiring a pet. But once a person makes that commitment a dog will give back a thousand times more love.

5.

Getting up in the morning I have a few set things I have to do to make sure my day goes well, and to help me wake up. I have to put in my contact lenses, because I am blind without them, and I need to get the kettle going. The hot water will make my coffee and my oatmeal. To get my dog going I have to pour her a half cup of dog food. She also needs a spoonful of my oatmeal. While I eat breakfast I go over a list of things I have to do. This is how I get myself going in

Introductory
Elements
EXERCISES

All introductory elements are separated by a comma EXCEPT prepositional phrases of less than five words. In that case, the comma is optional.

Introductory Elements
EXERCISES

The answers to these exercises are in the back of this book.

the morning.

6.

In the world of video games there are lots of online options for cooperative game play but my favorite is League of Legends. For one thing, this is a game with unlimited room to grow. There is no linear story so you can't reach the end, or fight a big, main boss. The difficulty is not in bigger and bigger bad guys. It comes from competing against human minds, because people are far more versatile and surprising than a computer ever could be.

7.

Learning about the history of the world, is fascinating, and is crucial to understanding how people came to be the way they are. For example the reason that Saint Patrick's Day is widely celebrated in the United States is due to the huge influx of Irish immigrants between 1820 and 1930. Those immigrants came to the US, because conditions in Ireland had become terrible. In fact there are currently more people of Irish descent living in the United States today than live in Ireland.

SEMICOLONS

This is a piece of punctuation that I see lots of students try to use. It's elegant and sophisticated, but it is often used incorrectly. The semicolon is used in two situations.

First, and more commonly, it is used in cases where you have two closely related thoughts, and you want to speed up the way they are read.

To do this, you must have an independent clause on both sides of the semicolon. I like to think of this like a teeter totter, and the independent clause is the big kid on the playground.

If a big kid and a little kid try to play on a teeter totter, it isn't any fun. The big kid keeps one side of the teeter totter down. There must be balance.

If you have a big kid on both sides, little kids can ride along, like dependent clauses and gerund phrases, and not affect the overall balance.

So that's the rule. You must have an independent clause (the big kid of any sentence) before and after the semicolon. If you are using a semicolon correctly, you could replace it with a period and the sentences would still be correct. You could also put in a comma and a coordinating conjunction, and it could be a correct compound sentence. If the coordinating conjunction is there, don't use the semicolon! Semicolons and coordinating conjunctions don't get along.

You choose to use a semicolon instead of a period and instead of a comma and a coordinating conjunction to stylistically show a close connection between the two ideas. It's cool. It's something you ought to get comfortable with and use to make an impression on your reader. Don't use it all the time. It's a special occasion kind of punctuation.

The second case in which we use a semicolon is when we make a list of items that already have a comma in the elements of the list. In that case, we are using the semicolon to be clear.

Here's an example:

> On the tour, The Clash will visit Atlanta, Georgia; Washington, D.C.; and Peoria, Illinois.

City and states already have a comma. Atlanta, Georgia is clear. We know that is how that is written. Now look at the same sentence without the semicolons:

8

The proper way to use a semicolon:
independent clause;
independent clause

Don't use a semicolon with a coordinating conjunction!

Use a semicolon when you make a list of items that have commas already.

SEMICOLONS

On the tour, The Clash will visit Atlanta, Georgia,
Washington, D.C., and Peoria, Illinois.

This version is confusing. Are they going to be in Washington and D.C.? There is definitely more than one Washington. In fact, there is more than one Georgia in the world and more than one Atlanta. If we were speaking, we would know the difference based on vocal inflection. In writing, we can't rely on that.

Without the semicolons, the reader isn't sure what the writer is trying to say, and the job of punctuation is to make written communication as clear as it can possibly be.

Want more on this? Go to madskillzacademics.com.

SEMICOLONS

1.

Everyone knows that dogs' noses are better than human noses; but not everyone understands how much better. For example a dog can smell a human being's feelings. When a person feels fear or anger or sorrow different hormones are released into the bloodstream. An increased heart rate drives the hormones to the surface of the skin and they are then passed through the skin in impossibly small amounts. However the amount coming off the skin is plenty to tell a dog everything it needs to know about the person's mood. Dogs can literally smell feelings; that's how good their noses are.

2.

In the event of a zombie apocalypse many people will be completely unprepared, and will immediately become part of the zombie problem. Consider how many people go to work sick; we can't even properly contain the spread of the common cold. That co-worker who gave the whole office the flu will someday turn the whole office into zombies. Some people walk around with surgical masks on; because they think this will protect them from other people's germs. They could not be more wrong, because surgical masks are designed to protect the patient from the surgeon's germs. Wearing a surgical mask would only be a good idea if we could get the zombies to wear them. Putting surgical masks on zombies, is a good way to get bit.

3.

When fall finally comes each year, and changes color of the leaves it is time for pumpkin spice everything to come out at every grocery store. Some people don't like pumpkin spice; they call people who do like pumpkin spice "basic". I beg to differ. Pumpkin spice is a mix of cinnamon, cloves, and nutmeg; these are the spices that human beings have craved for thousands of years. The Spanish government was willing to finance Columbus's voyage of exploration, because he

Semicolons

EXERCISES

There are five errors in each paragraph. Find and correct them. They could be anything we have covered so far.

Semicolons
EXERCISES

was looking for an easier route to the pumpkin spices. Marco Polo was also after spices when he spent years traveling eastward. Unlike Columbus Marco Polo actually found the spices. So if Marco Polo was basic; I am proud to be basic too.

Should a semicolon be there? Is there an independent clause before it? Is there an independent clause after it? Is there no coordinating conjunction between them?

4.

One of the reasons that it is so difficult for Americans to stay a healthy weight is because of evolution. For thousands and thousands of years people hunted and gathered, and went through parts of each year when food was scarce. Through this process, human being developed a taste for high-calorie foods. If they killed a mammoth; they were better off eating the layer of fat rather than sticking to only the lean muscle. So today, a delicious steak will have marbling. Fried food is high in calories so our starving ancestors love it. A thick slab of butter melting on a loaf of bread would have saved a whole tribe during the ice age. Unfortunately, we are no longer in danger of starving and eating as though we are leads to obesity.

5.

The word "holiday" comes from the words holy day. Initially, all the holidays people had were based on religious celebrations or rituals. During pre-Roman times people would celebrate the holy days like summer solstice. This day was holy because people at the time lacked scientific explanations for the season; so they gave religious, supernatural explanations to the natural occurrences they observed. When Christianity spread across Europe, their holy days were saint days. They would parade holy relics through the streets or they would do acts of penance. Interestingly enough it was forbidden to wage war on a holy day, so the Catholic Church expanded the number of holy days until the calendar was almost filled. Today, holidays are about getting off of work and good deals on mattresses. In the U.S. our holidays are political, the Fourth of July; religious, Christmas,

SEMICOLONS

and traditional, Thanksgiving. Not many of our holidays are holy anymore.

6.

When a person thinks of Italian food they are likely to imagine a plate of spaghetti with marinara sauce. However the foods that we think of as Italian did not originate in Italy. Noodles were invented in Asia; it was through trade that noodles were brought to Italy, where Italians fell in love with noodles, and made them a staple of their diet. Tomatoes are native to the Americas. When tomatoes traveled to Europe through Spanish Conquistadors, the Italians embraced the tomato completely, eventually incorporating it into many traditional dishes. Italian food reflects a culture open to outside influences and willing to try new things. And thank goodness they did, because lasagna is delicious.

7.

Humans are not the only animals able to influence the climate of the earth around them; because part of Siberia is known as the Mammoth Steppes. Today, it is windswept and frigid. Very little grows there, and few animals can survive the harsh conditions. However archeologists have discovered that thousands of years ago, the Mammoth Steppes were lush, and were home to a wide range of creatures and plants. As the mammoths rooted for forage, they dug up and aerated the soil; as they traveled, they dispersed seeds in their dung. In fact mammoth dung provided food and shelter to insects, so that insects provided food to birds and small rodents, and they provided food to larger predators. When the mammoths died out, a key part of that ecology was removed and the whole system collapsed.

The answers to these exercises are in the back of this book.

FRAGMENTS

Fragments are sentences that DON'T have an independent clause.

ways to make a fragment:

subject is missing
predicate is missing
only a dependent clause

Want more on this? Go to
madskillzacademics.com.

A sentence fragment is a group of words that looks like a sentence but isn't. A fragment isn't a sentence because it doesn't have an independent clause.

Sometimes this is because there is no subject:

Running down a side street with the cops on their tails.

Sometimes this is because there is no predicate:

The wonderful, powerful Master of Ceremonies and King of the Dance.

Sometimes there is a subject and a predicate and a subordinating conjunction. In this case, we have a dependent clause all by itself, and we know that a dependent clause cannot stand alone. So that is also a fragment.

If the bus stops at the next corner.

Fragments can sometimes be difficult to spot in an essay because the fragment makes sense with the sentences around it.

The Harry Potter exhibit is another example of how capitalism leads to alternate consumption models. Since people are willing to pay for experiences.

If you look at that second part alone, it is clearly a fragment.

Since people are willing to pay for experiences.

This is why proofreaders will sometimes read from the end to the beginning, sentence by sentence. It's a trick to help keep them from missing something because of meaning.

The trick to fragments is that you actually can use them. For effect. On purpose.

You can't do that accidentally. You have to know what you are doing. So if this is something that you aren't rock solid on, don't try to use fragments for effect. Work on eliminating them from your writing completely first.

FRAGMENTS

1.

I don't do yoga regularly and I am certainly not claiming to be knowledgeable enough to teach anyone yoga; but the yoga moves I know are great for my back. Because I spend a lot of time working at a desk. My back can get sore. If I spend a long time working at my computer, I will give myself a break to do child's pose. Sitting on my heels, leaning forward on the ground, and reaching my arms as far forward as I can. I can feel the tension in my back release. It is not a complete yoga routine but it is enough to energize me.

2.

A French Press is a great way to make coffee. Usually made from a glass beaker with a top and a plunger with a wire filter. A French Press allows the ground coffee beans to steep directly in hot water for four minutes. The flavor of the coffee beans, and also more of their caffeine are released this way. Then the plunger filters the grounds out of the coffee, and traps them at the bottom of the beaker. A French Press makes delicious, strong coffee and it avoids wasting paper filters the way a drip coffee maker does. Or even worse, plastic pods like a Keurig.

3.

Jazz music has made a fascinating journey through American history. It began in New Orleans as an extension of the marching bands that still exist there. And ended up in universities and museums. Often, these first jazz musicians were self-taught, and unable to read music; however, they were willing to take risks. They would compete against one another, improvising off standard songs while crowds cheered

There are five errors in each paragraph. Find and correct them. They could be anything we have covered so far.

Fragments
EXERCISES

You will sometimes have more than one way to fix an error. In these exercises, I have given you one answer, but other answers can also be equally correct.

for the winners. From New Orleans, Jazz spread to other parts of the country with Black communities. Chicago in particular. Also, Kansas City became an important incubator for great jazz musicians. The 1920s were known as the Jazz era, as rebellious youth looking for more expressive music flocked to jazz clubs. Later, Jazz inspired the Beat poets. People imitating beats became Beatniks and the youth imitating Beatniks became hippies. Today, Jazz is considered an intellectual's music, but, I believe it will return again as the music of the disaffected. America would not have the culture it has today without Jazz.

4.

Flannery O'Conner is an American author known best for her short stories. She is a fascinating person. Immensely talented and equally tragic. She lived with chronic disease and pain and she was a Catholic in overwhelmingly Baptist Georgia. Because of her health she lived with her mother and wrote as much as her disease would allow. Her writing style is called Southern Gothic. She was brilliantly dark and the difficulties of her life help to explain why. She unfortunately died young, but had a huge impact on American literature.

5.

There is an unfortunate myth in American culture that success is completely the result of hard work and talent. This leads us to believe that everyone who achieves wealth or fame deserves wealth or fame. Which leads us to treat them differently. Worse than that we believe anyone in poverty deserves poverty. Hard work and talent are certainly a part of the picture and no one is saying that they are

FRAGMENTS

irrelevant; however, plenty of people are wealthy. Because they were in the right place at the right time. A religious person might describe this as a blessing or grace. People are always getting things, good or bad, large or small, that they don't deserve. No child deserves to be born to drug addicted or abusive parents. No one deserves to battle with depression or disease. Conversely no one deserves to win the lottery.

6.

Frank Capra was one of the most successful directors Hollywood has ever known. There was a long period of time during which every movie he made became a hit. He was an Italian immigrant and he loved, and valued the American Dream. Many of his movies revolve around the belief in the basic decency of the common man. Because his movies were so optimistic some people thought they were too sentimental and corny. They created a phrase to describe his approach. Capra Corn. He called it something different for he considered it the optimism of the immigrant.

7.

There is a strange trend in movies these days; where bad guys are becoming the center of attention. For example, there are a large number of children now who adore Darth Vader. Dressing up like him and playing his part from the movie. They have somehow missed that Vader kills people. For no good reason. Darth Vader blew up a planet. This is who children are emulating; a mass murderer. Good guys are boring. Only because many people today have not experienced firsthand the effects of real life evil.

The answers to these exercises are in the back of this book.

RUN-ONS AND COMMA SPLICES

Many students tell me that a run-on sentence is a sentence that is too long. They will see a sentence that has three or four independent clauses in it, and they will call that a run-on sentence.

If that is what you were taught, hold on tight. I am about to blow your mind.

A run-on sentence has nothing to do with how long it is or how many clauses. A run-on sentence is not punctuated correctly.

That's it.

That's all there is to it.

Remember when I said that independent clauses have to have the right buffer between them? Take that buffer away, and you get a run-on.

Here, let me show you.

Run-on:
a sentence with two or more independent clauses that aren't punctuated correctly.

> The cat ate my homework my dog got it back.

This is a run on. It is two independent clauses without the proper punctuation—or punctuation and conjunction—between them.

How do we fix it? Get that buffer in there!

> The cat ate my homework. My dog got it back.
> The cat ate my homework, but my dog got it back.
> The cat ate my homework; my dog got it back.

All three of these approaches are correct. You get to choose the one that stylistically appeals to you more. There are other ways to fix run-ons besides these three, but these are the least invasive.

comma splice:
when two independent clauses have only a comma between them

Comma splices are a type of run-on sentence. In the case of a comma splice, instead of just cramming two independent clauses together, one lonely comma tries to link the two clauses. One poor little comma. These independent clauses are giant wrestlers, so a comma can't do it alone.

> My brother went to school to be an engineer, my father reluctantly paid for it.

Look at that little comma there! Straining! This is all too much for it!

The same three fixes apply.

> My brother went to school to be an engineer. My father reluctantly paid for it.

RUN-ONS AND COMMA SPLICES

My brother went to school to be an engineer, and my father
reluctantly paid for it.
My brother went to school to be an engineer; my father
reluctantly paid for it.

There you go.

This is the kind of issue that is easy to explain, but if it's your
issue, it's hard to overcome. So if this is your issue, you have to work
hard in order to start seeing it. You need to label clauses constantly.
In every exercise in this book, label the clauses. The more you do it,
the better you will get at it. If you stick with it, you will start seeing
the run-ons. That is the only way to improve.

Want more on this? Go to
madskillzacademics.com.

Run-ons and Comma Splices
EXERCISES

Each paragraph has five errors. Find and correct them. They could be anything we have covered so far.

1.

When combustion engine tractors were invented they were a huge improvement over the previous plowing methods. The new tractors moved quickly over a field. Plowing huge swaths of farmland in a fraction of the time. The previous method of plowing, however, was animal power. Suddenly, there were thousands of horses, mules, and oxen who no longer served a purpose, farmers couldn't feed animals who did nothing. Many farmers wanted to keep the animals in gratitude for the service they had performed but the government had other plans. The government actually created an animal destruction program, requiring farmers to turn over their animals for slaughter. Technology moved forward animals were left behind.

2.

Cookies come in many flavors and varieties. However there is one cookie that dominates in the United States, that is the chocolate chip cookie. A vanilla cookie dough with chunks of melted chocolaty goodness scattered throughout. Some people prefer their chocolate chip cookies crunchy and hard; they are wrong. Chocolate chip cookies should be crisp on the outside and gooey in the center. They are best served warm, when breaking the cookie in half leads to strings of melted chocolate reaching between the halves. They should be eaten with a tall glass of cold milk, and shared with family and friends.

3.

When the Romans invaded England they found a country of savages. The Romans came with elephants. Which the English had never seen before. The English considered the beasts magical monsters, the Romans exploited their fear. However it is never a good idea to underestimate savages, in one battle, the English used the fog to hide a field full of trip ropes designed to cripple the elephants.

4.

The Nile River was once the source of the most fertile farmland in the world. Egypt was an ancient powerhouse due to the wealth and power that the Nile provided. Every year, the Nile flooded, silty water spread out for miles. When the Nile returned to its banks it left behind rich new soil. Unfortunately modern technology came along, the Nile was dammed up to stop the flooding. It is interesting to note how damming the Nile corresponded with a decrease in

RUN-ONS AND COMMA SPLICES

Egypt's international stature. While there were certainly many other contributing factors to this decline. People constantly believe they are smarter than nature.

5.

The internet has transformed the ways that people work, play, and go to the bank. Because people no longer have to interact with other people in order to get what they want. Everything can be bought online. This is certainly convenient, however, this is also leading to greater and greater isolation. Humans are social, cooperative creatures, being alone too much is not good for us. In fact, various scientific studies have shown that isolated people suffer more heart disease, more depression, and die sooner. The internet may save people time in the line at the bank but if people are using the internet to avoid other people the internet is literally killing them.

6.

Different dog breeds were created for different jobs, it is sometimes shown in how they look. Dachshunds were bred to hunt badgers their legs are short to help them follow badgers into their burrows. They were also bred for toughness; when a dog is face first in a badger burrow the badger can scratch up the dog's face. Dachshunds were bred not to back down when this happened. That is why they are so stubborn. Miniature dachshunds were bred for similar reasons but they were intended to hunt smaller animals like rats. Now we race dachshunds, because their short legs make them very funny when they are running.

7.

Some people argue that religion is the cause of most of the wars in history, that argument is based entirely on not knowing history. In reality, most wars have been fought over resources before oil, people fought over rich farm lands, trade routes, and harbors. Getting access and control over these resources leads to national wealth and all nations want wealth enough to kill for it. Some nations, instead of fighting for control of resources, would fight raiding wars. Vikings, for example. They raided to take wealth, but eventually, even the Vikings switched to settling on the territory they conquered. While religion was occasionally used to inspire soldiers the reality is that people have always been more greedy than they have been faithful.

Run-ons and Comma Splices
EXERCISES

Remember: there are many ways to fix a run-on or comma splice. The difference between them comes down to your style.

In the answers to this section, I will give you one possible option. This is to keep the answers section simple.

If you see a run-on or a comma splice, know that the three corrections are all equally good.

The answers to these exercises are in the back of this book.

chapter

11

There-place
Their-belongs to them
they're- they are

its-belongs to it
it's-it is

weather-rain and sun
whether-choice

Let me tell you the story of English. A long time ago on an island far away, a group of people settled. Then they were invaded by people from far away who spoke a different language. Then those people were invaded by other people. Then the island was taken over. And each time a new group of people came in, the new language would blend with the old languages, and the rules of the old language would blend with the rules of the new language until English was made.

English is one of the most difficult languages to learn. Lucky for you, you learned it as a baby before you knew it was hard. Among the difficulties of English, we have a very odd way of spelling things.

Even with the invention of spell check, we aren't safe from misspelling. We have a whole bunch of words that sound alike but are spelled differently. At this point, most of the spelling mistakes you will make will be when you correctly spell a different word.

This is going to be a case of memorizing. Our brains betray us in this one. In writing, I'll often use the wrong form of "there" or "its." I have learned to go back and double check. This is especially useful on social media where these kinds of mistakes can make you look dumb.

There- location
Their-belongs to them
They're- they are.

Its-belongs to it
It's- it is.

This one screws people up because it breaks the rules we understand about possession. Apostrophe ess shows that something belongs to someone! The thing that helps me remember this is that it is following the rules of "self." If you add "self" to a word, you don't put an apostrophe. So itself. Its.

Weather happens in the sky.
Whether is a choice you make.

To is a preposition.
Too means also or more than enough.
Two is a number.

This is very easy to mix up—not because you don't know which is which, but because small words like this are easy for your eye to skip over.

COMMONLY MISSPELLED WORDS

Your- belongs to you
You're- you are.

The apostrophe goes to the contraction. The way I remember that is by thinking that contractions are stronger because they are two wods instead of one, so they beat off the other words to get the apostrophe.

then-orders things in time
than-compares things

wear-put on clothes
where-place

This is not at all a complete list of commonly misspelled words. Over time, you will learn to look for any situation where an incorrect word could slip in. Starting with these will train you to look for them.

Another mistake I see too often is using thru instead of through. Yes, the first spelling makes more sense, and is used commonly in social media and text-speak, where it is fine, but in college, we spell it the hard way. In fact, if this is hard for you, it's because you have trained yourself to use "thru" too thoroughly. The fix is to start writing out "through" in your text messages, too.

I know! So uncool! Ultimately, though, which is cooler: texting your friends or getting your college degree? The correct answer is college degree.

Remember that the way you speak to your friends would not be appropriate to use with your professor, so the way you write to your friends is not appropriate with a professor.

Your- belongs to you
You're- you are.

then-orders things in time
than-compares things

wear-put on clothes
where-place

Thru--NO
through--yes!

Want more on this? Go to madskillzacademics.com.

Commonly Misspelled Words
EXERCISES

Each paragraph has five errors. Find and correct them. They could be anything we have covered so far.

1.

Eating many different kinds of fruit is a good thing to do; however their are drawbacks. Take oranges, for example. Oranges are delicious, and are full of vitamin C. Once people have peeled an orange, they're hands will smell like orange for a while. Those who like the smell of oranges won't be to worried about this. For others, it is a real concern.

2.

I am a dog person, that is very clear from how I talk about dogs. I don't like cats, because I am allergic to them. Weather you are a dog person or a cat person, kittens and puppies are irresistible. I will pet kittens even though they make my eyes swell shut, and give me days of sinus problems. They're to cute to resist.

3.

Video games have gone mainstream, everyone is a gamer these days. Their are two major categories of video games. Console games are the games that require a special machine to play. Nintendo, Play Station, and X -box are all examples of gaming consoles. The other type of game are PC games those are the games that are played on a personal computer. This can be done by buying a game on a DVD, downloading it from Steam, or connecting to servers to play online. Like League of Legends. People tend to prefer to play one way or the other but the important thing is that these are games; they are supposed to be fun.

4.

In shopping for a new apartment there are many factors to consider. One factor that can impact quality of life greatly is which floor the apartment is on. Will their be neighbors above stomping around at all hours of the night? If the sound control in the building is good it's

COMMONLY MISSPELLED WORDS

not too much of a concern. If the sound control is bad; however, its like having a terrible roommate who never pays.

5.

I get it, grammar and punctuation are not you're favorite subjects. They're not mine, either. I love reading and writing so I need to know more about proofreading. In every person's professional life writing well will be essential at some point. When that moment comes be ready. Proofreading is like grooming your words. You wouldn't go into a professional setting wearing muddy clothes and with birds nesting in your hair. Don't send your words in that way.

6.

These days, it seems like everything is bad for you. Because the news is always looking for something else to scare you. However the way people are interpreting this can be a bit overblown. I was in a Target store once and I overheard a woman talking to an associate about a particular kind of sweetener she was looking for. She was getting angry that she couldn't find what she was looking for. She waved at the whole shelf of sweeteners and said, "This is all poison!" I wanted to point out to her that she apparently didn't know what poison is. She was very upset, she was scared. Someone had convinced her that it was life or death to change her sweetener and she believed it.

7.

Are you trying to achieve a goal? If so, picture your goal like a mountain you must climb. Because you begin at the bass of the mountain climb with porpoise. Check the whether before you climb, or your going to be sorry. In this case, that means be aware of what is going on in the world. Don't set a goal to be a telephone operator in the era of cell phones. That is a goal you cannot achieve.

Commonly
Misspelled Words
EXERCISES

The answers to these exercises are in the back of this book.

QUESTION MARKS

You know this piece of punctuation. You are probably wondering why I bring it up at all. Of course you know what a question mark is. You know what it does.

But there is one small but important distinction that you need to pay close attention to.

Question marks are used to indicate DIRECT questions.

> Is that for sale?
> Who shot J.R.?
> Why is my foot on fire?

Question marks are NOT used in INDIRECT questions.

> I wonder if that is for sale.
> I think about who shot J.R.
> Rosa asked me why my foot is on fire.

Do you see the difference? A direct question is actually asking a question. An indirect question is not.

That's the big question mark error I see in student essays. There are a few other minor issues that can come up related to question marks in things like tag questions, but those issues are highly unlikely to occur in college level writing.

Isn't this easy?

direct question = ?

indirect question=
no ?

Want more on this? Go to
madskillzacademics.com.

QUESTION MARKS

1.

Why does American culture have a problem with aging? While a few male movie stars last into their later years most of the stories Hollywood tells are about young people? Billions of dollars are spent every year trying to hide or fight the signs of aging. With creams from goat placenta, lasers for the skin, pills with hormones and anti-oxidants. All of this time and money are spent fighting a natural and inevitable process. Aging is encoded in human DNA. Their is no escaping it; embracing it is the only option. So why don't we.

2.

Many people wonder why we keep pets? They are expensive, dirty, and needy, Americans spend billions of dollars a year on them. For those people who have pets the answer is simple. The love we feel for our animals. However there are other benefits. Petting a dog or a cat has been scientifically shown to reduce high blood pressure and stress, and reducing these can lead to longer, healthier human lives.

3.

Depression is a serious problem. People of every race, gender, and religion suffer from it. Is it just a form of sadness? No, its a neurological chain reaction that can be exhibited in many ways; through disconnection, pain, or a general lack of energy. Some people think that a person can power through depression, they say that a depressed person needs to get up and go. This attitude does not help. Depression is a result of brain chemistry we are only just beginning to understand and we all need to respect that. Science can't cure the common cold, either, but is anyone telling people with sniffles that it's all in their heads.

4.

The Cherokee are a tribe of Native Americans who once lived in Georgia and South Carolina. Unlike other Native Americans the Cherokee were not hunters and gatherers. They were farmers with towns. When the English introduced writing to the New World, the Cherokee quickly adopted it, creating their own alphabet and print-

Question Marks
EXERCISES

Each paragraph has five errors. Find and correct them. They could be anything we have covered so far.

Question Marks
EXERCISES

Don't forget to space out these exercises. You will have better long term retention working at something for short periods of time over many days than you will by working at something for a couple of hours once.

The answers to these exercises are in the back of this book.

ing newspapers and books, there was even a translation of the Bible in Cherokee. However white settlers coveted Cherokee land. Though the Cherokee had an elected government, the US government bribed the brother of the Cherokee president to sign a resettlement treaty. Although the brother had no authority to represent the Cherokee. Is this fair. Then, the US military forced thousands of Cherokee to walk from Georgia to Oklahoma. Many people died along the way. This walk is what we now know as the Trail of Tears.

5.

Which is a better pet, a dog or a cat. It depends on what you want from a pet. Do you want unconditional love, loyalty, and devotion? Or do you prefer an aloof animal that poops in your house. Do you like your pet to be trainable, and able to learn cool tricks? Like catching a Frisbee. Or do you want your pet to ignore you. Clearly dogs have a lot of great things to offer. If neither of these options appeals to you, you can always get a fish.

6.

Peaches can either be cling peaches or freestone. Cling peaches are where the peach hangs on tight to the stone in the center and its hard to cut away the peach flesh. The other kind falls easily away, as it is cut open. Cling peaches are fine if a person eats a peach like an apple but if a person is making a pie the other kind is better. Trying to slice cling peaches into nice wedges is frustrating and horrible. Because I end up mangling the peach every time.

7.

What is the meaning of life? Questioning the meaning of our lives, seems to be a fundamentally human thing to do. Because the answer to the question gives us a sense of purpose. Otherwise we feel lost in chaos. There is more than one answer to the question. Is it possible that we don't need the answer. Is it possible that we just need to ask the question.

QUOTATION MARKS

Quotation marks exist to indicate that the words inside it are the exact words that someone said. In most academic writing, those words would belong to a source you are using. In creative or narrative writing, you would use that to indicate what people said to each other.

Our first concern is the DIRECT quotation versus the INDIRECT quotation. This works the same way as it does for quotation marks. Are these the exact words? Then you need quotation marks.

Juan said, "I want a pizza."
"All men are created equal" are the words that democracy is built on.
"This situation is unfair," my opponent insists.

Indirect quotations are when you are talking about what someone said without using their exact words. These do not get quotation marks.

Juan said that he wants a pizza.
The idea that people are all equal is what democracy is built on.
My opponent insists that this situation is unfair.

The key word for indirect quotations is the word "that." But then you have to remember that the word "that" can be invisible.

Juan said he wants a pizza.

Eeeek! Pay attention to this.

There are a few other reasons that a writer might want to use quotation marks. Sometimes it can be to indicate that a word or phrase would be used by others in what you are discussing.

The people playing the game might refer to this as "AFK."

Or that the word you are using is from a foreign language, which can also be indicated with italics.

The citizens of Mexico City would buy "dulces" to celebrate the holiday.

Items in quotes can be treated like lists of phrases or things people have said. In that case, the commas will be exactly like any other list.

They said things like "Leave me alone" and "I hate you!"
The crowd murmured, "Yes," "That sounds good," and "I agree."

Or you can put quote marks around words to make them stand out if they are not meant to be part of the meaning of the sentence, like I am doing in this when I discuss words. I could also use italics. But I chose quote marks, and I must stay consistent.

The key word for indirect quotations is
the word "that." But then you have to remember
that the word "that" can be invisible.

If you want to use slang, just use slang. It's cool. No quote marks needed. It is more important that you be aware of the effect of that slang word on your reader.

Students love to put quote marks around slang. The most common use of quote marks is to indicate that these are the exact words spoken or written, often by someone other than the writer. If the slang you are using is the word you want to use, then just use it. You don't need quote marks. In formal writing, quote marks do not mean you are being sarcastic or mocking something. In formal writing, they only indicate that these are someone else's words.

DIALOGUE

Quotation marks are going to come in handy as you write academic papers and you quote different sources. But you might also write a narrative essay or a short story, and then, quotation marks become vital to use in dialogue.

When you are writing dialogue, we have a lot of punctuation to take into consideration.

"Hello," James Bond said.

Look closely at the end of the quotation. First we have a comma, and then we have the end quote mark. The comma stands in for a period. But what if the quote uses something else?

"Hello!" James Bond said.

The exclamation point is still inside the quotation mark.

James Bond said, "Hello."

QUOTATION MARKS

In this case, the comma is outside the quotation mark. Because the tag (the part of the sentence that tells us who is speaking) is in front of the quote.

However, let's say the sentence around the quotation is asking a question.

Did James Bond say, "Hello"?

So if the quotation is a question, the question mark goes inside the quotation marks, and if the sentence outside the quotation is asking the question, the question mark goes outside the quotation marks.

When you are writing dialogue, every time someone new speaks, you should have a paragraph break, no matter how short the paragraph. This is a convention we have in writing to make it clear who is talking.

James said, "Hello, Goldfinger."
Goldfinger said, "You found my secret lair. Bravo."
"I am going to take you to jail." James lit a cigarette. "Pack a suitcase. You are going away for a long time."
"Or am I?"

Who said that last line? Goldfinger did, and we know that because it is a new paragraph.

Another error I see often is treating everything inside the quote marks as one long sentence. Sentences inside the quote mark need to be punctuated the way that they would be without quotation marks. You can have several sentences inside the same quote marks. What matters is only that the sentences are said by the same person.

James said, "I'd like a martini. I always order martinis. Heck, this is a very good martini!"

I know this adds up to a lot of rules, and if this isn't something you are familiar with, it can seem overwhelming. If you find this difficult, read more modern fiction. The more you see this, the more it makes sense. Like all of the rules we are studying, they exist to help make things clearer to the reader.

punctuating dialogue

1. Punctuate sentences inside quote marks the same as you would outside. You can have multiple sentences inside quote marks.
2. Here in the US, we use double quote marks
3. New speaker equals new paragraph.
4. The tag (he said, she said) can go before or after the quote.
5. Read more.

Want more on this? Go to madskillzacademics.com.

QUOTATION MARKS

Each paragraph has five errors. Find and correct them. They could be anything we have covered so far.

1.

Have you ever heard anyone say, "I'm a dog person." or "I'm a cat person?" It's interesting that people like their pets enough to make that part of there identity. You don't hear people say, "I'm a cheese person" or "I'm a cotton person" with the same level of conviction. There are some things we like that don't matter but there are other things that become part of who we are.

2.

I overheard a lady in Starbucks ask "if they were going to make pumpkin spice last all year long?" I wonder the same thing. The barista said I don't know. As I thought about it, I decided that the answer should be no. Having pumpkin spice as a seasonal thing keeps it special. If we had it year round it would become nothing special and it is nice to have something be special.

3.

My mother was in Florida during Hurricane Matthew. Before it hit, she wrote me a text that said goodbye. If I don't make it remember that I love you. I wrote back, "You aren't going to die. This is America." After the hurricane, I learned that "the worst thing that happened was she lost her cable." However, there was another person who did die, that person had a heart attack and EMT couldn't get there in time because of the storm.

4.

When children are small they love to ask questions. "Why is the sky blue?" "Why do dogs have tails and people don't"? "Where does the water go when it goes down the drain?" For the adults living with small children it can get frustrating to answer so many questions. When they don't know the answers. When children stop asking

QUOTATION MARKS

questions, they start the process of conforming so we need to help everyone ask more questions.

5.

The kids today say "on fleek." This means that something is "cool." It used to be, that other words were used to mean this same thing. Michael Jackson sang a song in which "bad" meant "good." That's how people are, they want to be special. Each new wave of young people comes up with a new way of saying the same old thing. They like to confuse the adults and special slang makes them feel like they belong. But eventually all these on fleek kids will grow up to be adults who just don't get it.

6.

I was walking down the street when I heard someone yell, Hey! It was my friend. He told me that, "he had been yelling at me for three blocks." I apologized for not hearing him, however, that's the way I am. When I am walking along lost in my own thoughts; I don't hear anything going on around me. The nice thing is I don't notice street vendors but I wish I could do better at hearing my friends.

7.

     "No" she said. "he can't come in, I am not ready".

     Her mother said "that he has been waiting.

     "Let him wait!" she cried, "He deserves worse."

     "No."

The answers to these exercises are in the back of this book.

14

Verb must match the subject in number (singular or plural)and person (first, second, third)

I am

not

I is
I are
I be

SUBJECT-VERB AGREEMENT

When a noun and a verb form a relationship known as a clause, the verb transforms itself to fit the noun. The verb changes to express TIME (did this thing happen in the past, the future, or the future), PERSON (first--I, second--you, or third—he, she, it) and NUMBER (singular or plural). When we talk about subject-verb agreement, we are talking about the predicate matching the noun in number and person.

This is one of those things that a native speaker of English picks up as a toddler. I is or I am? One of these should sound wrong to you.

So why are we covering it? Reason number one: some of you didn't grow up with Standard English. You say, "Where you be at?" instead of "Where are you?" Like I said before, there's nothing wrong with language that expresses meaning to another person since that is the whole and only point to any language, but you need to use the language that is appropriate to college. Does it feel odd or false? I don't like dressing up for weddings, but I do it. If this is a topic that interests you, you should read about code switching and language politics. I am only here to tell you to do it.

The second and much more important reason that we are covering this is that sometimes, the subject-verb agreement isn't so clear. The subject and the predicate can be separated by other words and phrases, causing confusion, or the subject can be a compound subject, which causes some special rules to kick in.

Take this sentence:

> The reason for the extensive expeditions is that
> there is much to learn.

The subject LOOKS like "expeditions." It is closer to the predicate and it makes sense. But it is not the subject. It can't be because of the word "for."

What? "For" in this sentences is working as a preposition, and prepositions are followed by nouns that belong to them, called the object of the preposition, and the object of the preposition can NEVER be the subject of the sentence.

Think of it like monogamy. If the noun is in a relationship with a preposition, it can't be in a relationship with a verb, and vice versa.

The subject of the sentence is reason. What potentially makes this sentence confusing is that "reason" is singular and "Expeditions" is plural, and so if we aren't paying attention, we make the predicate

SUBJECT-VERB AGREEMENT

agree with "expeditions" and now we have a problem.

This is why we started with parts of speech and clauses. If you need to go back and review, do it.

What about those compound subjects?

If you have a compound subject linked with "and", then you treat the whole thing as plural, no matter what the individual parts are.

John and Susan are starting a new business.

You might be thinking that this is too obvious and that you would never have a problem with this, but again, when more words get into the sentence, it becomes murkier.

The online division of a a multinational corporation and Susan with the help of a large loan are starting a new business.

If you have a compound subject linked with "or", you use whichever subject comes last.

Either John or Susan is starting a new business.
Either John or seven dogs are starting a new business.
Either seven dogs or Susan is starting a new business.

This is a more arbitrary rule that you'll have to learn rather than recognize. It doesn't come strictly from usuage. But it also doesn't come up very often.

AND=plural
OR= use the last option

Want more on this? Go to madskillzacademics.com.

Subject-Verb Agreement
EXERCISES

Each paragraph has five errors. Find and correct them. They could be anything we have covered so far.

1.

Whales are amazing creatures. A family of whales travel thousands of miles every year; in order to mate and to follow the food supply. They communicate with each other through complicated songs. Their are many different kinds of whales with very different characteristics but linking them all together is their immense size. No animal on land can match them; the water supports their large bodies, and provides them with enough food to maintain body mass in a way that land creatures struggle to match.

2.

As medical science advances, we are discovering that one of the worst things that can happen to our bodies are stress. Stress is associated with high blood pressure, heart disease, and even cancer. How is a person in this modern world supposed to avoid stress. The problem is that our stress systems are designed to work well in fight or flight situations and we are hardly ever in fight or flight situations anymore. The chemicals that would be very useful in trying to outrun a saber-toothed tiger is not at all useful in dealing with a demanding boss. With the tiger, the body would be flooded, action would be taken, and the danger would pass. Because the person was eaten. A quick flash of adrenaline works great. Low doses of adrenaline week after week is a killer.

3.

Stringed instruments have been around for thousands of years. For most of that time vinyl wasn't an option. Strings were made instead from animal intestine stretched tight and dried. This explains a line from Shakespeare that says, "Amazing that cat guts can hew men's souls." It lead one to wonder how people discovered that sound could be made from animal entrails? Possibly early people were drying intestine to eat later. A process that they would be using on animal meat. Perhaps the intestine were stretched on a drying rack, when someone brushed against it.

4.

SUBJECT-VERB AGREEMENT

A group of horses run down a hill, a bird twitters in an old oak tree. Tall grasses waving lazily in the sun calls out to you to come lay down and relax. An old wooden fence invites you too hop over; a spring burbles happily along. This could be your happy place. Its always free to visit in your mind.

5.

Today, when people discuss race, they often fall back on imprecise language and bad definitions, this leads to confusion. What is the "white" race. In reality, there is no such thing as white as a race, it is a classification that includes many races and it changes all the time. For example, Irish people, for the vast majority of human history, was not white. Nor were Italians, Spaniards, Hungarians, Russians, Germans, or Polish people considered white. Now they are. This is why "white history month" is not an idea worth entertaining.

6.

While dogs or a cat is a typical pet in the United States of America. Their are many other animals capable of being pets. Ferrets are a rodent similar to a weasel that can learn to come when called. It is illegal to keep ferrets in California, because they can get loose and become pests. Many people keep birds. Parrots can live for sixty years; so a person would not have to suffer the loss of that pet. However, parrots are noisy and annoying. Fish are an easy pet that will never learn their names or come when they are called. Clearly any other pet that people might keep in their homes are not as good.

REMEMBER:
The object of the preposition is never the subject of the sentence.

7.

Before paper, people used other things to write messages and keep records. An alphabet based on a series of wedge shapes were the first writing. Cuneiform was pressed into clay, and then dried. Europeans wrote on parchment. Specially prepared animal skins. Oftentimes people would scrape the old writing off and reuse them over and over. To this day, a diploma is called a sheep skin, because the earliest diplomas were recorded this way.

The answers to these exercises are in the back of this book.

15

it=singular
anyone= singular
each=singular
everybody=singular
me=singular

PRONOUN-ANTECEDENT AGREEMENT

Boy! Doesn't that sound scary? Pronoun-antecedent agreement! It has a fancy name, so it must be crazy difficult!

Stop right there. Don't let big words intimidate you.

Pronoun: we know what this is. It is a word that stands in for a noun. He, she, it, they, who, that, and so on.

Antecedent: this literally means the thing that comes before. A pronoun stands in for a noun. The noun it stands in for is there in the writing. The noun always comes before the pronoun. That's how we make things clear.

If I walked up to you and said, "She killed it," you would be completely confused, and maybe a little scared. That's because this sentence has two pronouns, she and it, but I didn't give you the antecedent for either pronoun which means that I never said the nouns these pronouns are standing in for.

So I could be saying that your mother murdered your dog, or I could be saying that Simone Biles just did an amazing trick on the balance beam. You have no idea without the antecedent.

Now, what we mean by agreement is that the pronoun has to match the noun it stands in for. And it must match in gender and number. Look at this:

The man ran. It needed to escape.

What is happening? If I intended "it" to stand in for the man, I have created a pronoun-antecedent agreement problem. Because "man" should match "he," not "it."

The man ran. He needed to escape.

There. That is clear and understandable. And remember, that's our goal in writing, to be clear and understandable.

I know what you are thinking. You would never make a mistake like this. True. It is highly unlikely that a native speaker of English would ever make this mistake. However, you might make a mistake matching the other category: number.

The stars are so beautiful once you get out away
from the city. I love looking at it.

"It" cannot represent "the stars" because "stars" are plural and "it" is singular.

PRONOUN-ANTECEDENT AGREEMENT

Or how about this one:

> A folder should be given to every student. They
> should keep that folder through the whole class.

"Student" is singular. "They" is plural. This is a grammatical quirk people do to avoid using "he or she". I get it. "He or she" is clunky. And some people think that the language will change until "they" means "singular individual who is of indeterminate gender." But that day is not today. So learn to do it right. Your grade will thank you.

If you want to avoid "he or she," change the antecedent.

> A folder should be given to all students. They
> should keep that folder through the whole class.

The other scenario you have to look out for is when pronouns stand in for lists grouped by "or." Much like with subject verb agreement, if we have singular items listed with an "or":

> Susan or Maria
> Left or right

then they will be represented by a singular pronoun. If the second item is plural, then they will both be represented by a plural pronoun.

> Susan or ten long-haired Chihuahuas
> They left hair on the couch.

Pronoun antecedent agreement issues also crop up when the sentences are long and there is more distance between the pronoun and the antecedent. But if you are a native speaker of English, your ear has already been trained to catch that. Remember when you were little and you spent literally all of your time babbling? That was when you were doing the hard work of learning the rules of language. What we are doing now is becoming aware of what we already know.

I find students will often sense that something is wrong with a sentence, but not be able to put their finger on exactly what it is, and it is usually a pronoun-antecedent agreement problem.

So keep an eye out for it. If this is something you have issues with, try reading your writing aloud. When you read aloud, pronoun-antecedent agreements become more obvious.

AND=plural
OR= use the last option

Want more on this? Go to madskillzacademics.com.

Pronoun-Antecedent Agreement
EXERCISES

Each paragraph has five errors. Find and correct them. They could be anything we have covered so far.

1.

My niece picked out a special gift to send to my dog; a Wonder Woman costume with a flouncy red skirt. She loved it. I put it on her, as soon as I got it in the mail. It was too small, and my dog is a Dachshund, so the skirts wrapped around her chest. I had to call my sister immediately and tell her that "my dog loved the gift." Actually, my dog acted as though this costume had destroyed her will to live. She refused to move until I had taken them off.

2.

Lights are measured on a color scale that is defined by degrees. An incandescent light bulb is 3600 degrees. Which on camera is an orange light. Sunlight, specifically the light between the hours of ten in the morning and four in the evening, is 5600 degrees. They are blue. Actually the color changes from dawn to midday. The human eye and human brain are able to adapt to the change in light color without disrupting vision, but a person can train themselves to see these differences. Cameras need special technology called white balance to adapt to see it.

3.

When a person reaches a certain age, they begin to take on the responsibilities of adulthood. Starting with living alone. In America, this particular step is often taken by going to college, or moving in to an apartment with roommates. These first apartments, rented in a bad part of town and poorly maintained, is usually inexpensive, crowded, and dirty. To an eighteen-year-old, having a couch on the front lawn seems cool, to an adult, it looks like a great way to destroy a couch.

4.

The massive growth in the Chinese economy has been fueled largely by Chinese piracy. China does not respect copyrights or patents. While the Chinese auto industry has been booming, the cars they produce are almost entirely copies of car designs from other countries. Their is a chain of coffee shops that is a copy of Starbucks.

PRONOUN-ANTECEDENT AGREEMENT

In Chinese cities, one of the most popular stores are a copy of the Apple Store. If China was constrained by the laws that govern other countries, and if they compensated the people who created the items they enjoy, their growth would be slower.

5.

Winter is a time to forget about fashion and dress to survive. Especially in more northern cities like Chicago. A person in Chicago will wear the warmest things they can find. Several shirts or a jacket keeps a person warm in brisk whether but when it gets really cold outside, very few people can manage to layer enough. A snow suit with puffy sleeves and seven scarves are barely enough.

6.

When a man or a woman apply for a job, studies have shown that men are far more willing to exaggerate their skills, and far less likely to suffer for it. A woman, on the other hand, due to the pressures of society, will mostly apply for jobs only when they have all the qualifications the announcement asks for. Studies have also shown that in the workplace, people assume a man is qualified until he proves that he is not, while people will assume a woman is not qualified until she proves that she is. Consequently men tend to progress more quickly in their careers.

7.

When stories hit a collective psychological chord in humanity, it gets passed on from generation to generation. It's for this reason that early psychologists like Sigmund Freud were able too identify many modern psychological dysfunctions using Ancient Greek mythology. For example, the Oedipus Complex is an issue in which a man becomes fixated on his own mother, creating barriers to his growth. The name comes from a Greek play about a man named Oedipus who killed his father and married his mother but we see a modern example of this story in *Psycho*. In that movie, Norman Bates has no father, and is so fixated on his mother that he keeps her dead body. Due to his fixation he is trapped in a juvenile state.

EXERCISES

We've covered a lot at this point. Reviewing these paragraphs is a lot like real proofreading now.

The answers to these exercises are in the back of this book.

TITLES

There are two categories of titles. I like to call them big things and little things. Big things are novels, movies, album titles. Little things are stories, essays, poems, songs. Big things often contain little things.

The titles of big things are italicized. If italics are not available, like in hand writing, then you underline instead. We do this because underlining was code to printers back in the day to italicize. So underlining means, "I wish I could italicize this."

The titles of little things get quote marks around them. That's the only option.

Titles of books, movies, albums, works of visual art are italicized.

Titles of articles, poems, short stories, songs have quote marks around them.

Big Things

"Little Things"

Titles are also capitalized according to special rules. The first word and last word are always capitalized. The other words are capitalized UNLESS the words are prepositions or articles.

You remember prepositions and articles from Parts of Speech, but if you need to go back and review, do it.

So if I wrote a book and decided to use the sentence, "My dad knows nothing about the Force" as the title, it would look like this:

My Dad Knows Nothing about the Force

Capitalize:
The first word
The last word
All other words except
prepositions and articles

"About" is a preposition and "the" is an article. Everything else is capitalized. This is the title of a book, a big thing, which means we italicize it.

One big exception to this rule is the Bible. It is not italicized, and the books of the Bible are not italicized nor do they have quote marks around them.

Other exceptions to italicizing (but not the capitalization rules) are the titles of legal documents like the Constitution, titles of computer software like Microsoft Word, and the title of your own paper. But remember, the capitalization rules do apply.

Want more on this? Go to
madskillzacademics.com.

TITLES

1.

The Harry Potter books were incredibly popular, when they first came out. Release dates for Harry Potter and The goblet of Fire featured parties and kids dressed up. At midnight, bookstores would open to hoards of eager children carrying wands and sales were through the roof. Since then, no book has come close. While Twilight and "The Hunger Games" were also popular they didn't create the same kind of frenzy that Harry Potter did.

2.

In the poem Stopping by woods on a Snowy Evening by Robert Frost, the speaker is returning home one evening, and ponders the landscape. It's "the darkest evening of the year" he says. Technically, the darkest evening of the year is winter solstice. It is the time when the planet has tilted the North Pole as far away from the sun as possible in it's current orbit. Ancient cultures often associated this with mystical or religious rites.

3.

As an American, I am accustomed to a certain quality of entertainment. But I sometimes enjoy television made by Canadians or Brits. One excellent show from the Canadians is Orphan Black. It is a science fiction drama with excellent acting. Though occasionally the writing isn't that great. British television shows like Sherlock and Top Gear have become popular in the U.S. However, a British

Titles
EXERCISES

Each paragraph has five errors. Find and correct them. They could be anything we have covered so far.

Titles
EXERCISES

television show has such short seasons that they feel more like appetizers then a full meal.

One issue with setting up exercises with titles is that you need to know what kind of thing is titled, so I have added that information into the paragraphs. This is not how a person normally would write this.

4.

One of the most famous paintings in the world is the Mona Lisa. It is a portrait of a woman with her hands folded. This woman has captured many imaginations. Their is a song called Mona Lisa, a poem called Mona Lisa, and a movie called Mona Lisa smiles.

5.

Christopher Marlow was an English playwright who lived at the same time as Shakespeare, he was a hot shot who had a few big hits early in his career. His most famous play was Doctor Faustus. He also wrote poetry, including The Passionate Shepherd to his Love. Some people think Marlow was the true author of Shakespeare's plays, Henry VI. Marlowe was a trouble maker. He drank hard and slept with married women, and might have been a spy. He was killed in a knife fight when he was only 29 years old.

6.

There is a line from a song by Eminem called lose Yourself from the movie Eight mile that actually exposes a big issue with the welfare system in the US. He raps "Man/ these goddamn/ food stamps /don't buy diapers." This is true, food stamps cannot be used to buy diapers. For some reason, the government has classified diapers as luxuries. As a result of this policy, it is not uncommon for the children of the

TITLES

very poor to not wear diapers. Social workers report parents using paper towels or plastic bags. Because plastic bags are an unacceptable alternative, these parents are at risk of losing thier children. To be on food stamps, a person must demonstrate they're in poverty. They cannot have savings or a reasonable income. So where does the government imagine they are going to get the money for diapers.

7.

One of my favorite shows is "Supernatural." Its in season 12 now; that is a huge achievement for a television show. In this show, Dean and Sam are brothers who hunt ghosts and monsters. Many of the writers on this show came from the X-Files, the greatest science fiction show of all time. Supernatural is a fun show but it doesn't quite meet the levels achieved by that show.

EXERCISES

The answers to these exercises are in the back of this book.

POSSESSIVE NOUNS

In English, if we want to show possession, we add 's to the end of the word that owns something.

> Dad's cookies
> Batman's car
> shoe's laces.

If the owner is plural and ends in ess, then we add just '.

> Seven dogs' tails.
> All the cars' bumpers.

If the plural form of a word doesn't end in s, then we go back to 's

> Children's stories.

word doesn't end in an s= 's
word does end in an s= ' or 's

If the singular form of the word ends in an s, you can go either way. The Gross's house or The Gross' house.

Pay attention! This is an easy one to overlook!

I see students make errors on this based on carelessness. Pay attention to possessive nouns because the difference between the dog's tails and the dogs' tails is huge. In the first one, you have found a dog with multiple tails! That's strange and amazing! And probably not what you meant.

This is one of those rules that is so simple that everyone gets it. However, we are building up a lot of rules here, and this little one can get lost in the shuffle if you aren't careful.

Want more on this? Go to madskillzacademics.com.

POSSESSIVE NOUNS

1.

In "A Tale of Too Cities," a book by Charles Dickens, the two cities in the title are London and Paris. The cities problems are different but connected; London is corrupt, while Paris is overcome by the madness of the French Revolution. The ending of the book is one of hope, though. That hope is provided through love and immense personal sacrifice, these are the tools good people have to fight with.

2.

They're is no sound I like better than the sound of my dogs' snores. It is a sound that tells me that she is safe and content; which I care about a great deal. I do not enjoy anyone else's snoring, it usually makes me think that, "A person might have sleep apnea."

Each paragraph has five errors. Find and correct them. They could be anything we have covered so far.

3.

Writing for an academic audience can be daunting. Much of the academic writing that exists is dense, and filled with jargon. However even academic writing ought to be clear. When an author sits down to write, they don't think I hope no one understands me. The authors' ideas need clarity in order to spread, and spreading ideas is one main purpose of writing.

4.

Three birds sat on a wire, waiting for a car to come along under them. One man saw them waiting, and decided to chase them off. The man got a flame thrower out of his garage. The birds stared at him until he pulled the trigger. The three birds tails feathers caught on fire and they flew away squawking. The mans' flame thrower caught on fire. He was not supposed to have them, so he went to jail.

5.

My dog is good at begging. When she wants something, she stands near and looks up at me. A dogs' eyes are a powerful thing. Big and brown and sad. She looks up at me, and starts making small, sad sounds. Does she not have a treat? Am I heartless. When her misery becomes too great, she rests her chin on my knee. She is too miserable to lift it. If only someone would give her a treat. She might have a chance. I try to remember that she is a fat little dog and needs to lose weight. She clearly believes she is starving.

6.

Juan, Klaus, and a group of children shared a basket of apples. What happened to Juans' apples. He made a pie. With Klauss apples he made a sauce. The childrens' apples were eaten right away. The children's apple cores were thrown into a trash can, weather they were finished or not.

7.

Their was a time when the bald eagle was at the edge of extinction; heavy pesticide use caused the shells of the eagles eggs to thin, and they would be easily damaged before the egg could hatch. Bald eagle numbers in the United States dwindled down to almost nothing

POSSESIVE NOUNS

but conservationists went to work. Lobbying for restrictions on pesticides and outlawing the sale of eagle feathers, helped turn the tide. Bald eagles made an amazing comeback. On June 28, 2007, they were removed from the endangered species list.

Possessive Nouns
EXERCISES

The answers to these exercises are in the back of this book.

CAPITALIZATION

There are dozens of rules for capitalization. You know the big ones: capitalize the first word in a sentence and people's names.

I see a few places that students tend to struggle. We will cover those here, but this is not a comprehensive list.

Let me say that again. There are more rules than what we will cover here!

Family Members

This is where I see students struggle most often. "Mom" is both a name and a relationship. Names get capitalized. Relationships do not.

How can you tell the difference? "My mom" is a relationship. "Mom" is a name. The possessive "my" indicates that this is a relationship.

> I will tell my mom that you are coming.
> I will tell Mom that you are coming.

This applies to your mom, his mom, and their mom, as well as dad, grandma, uncle, and so on.

Times of the Year

You capitalize months, days, and the names of specific holidays but not seasons. So Independence Day, January, and Tuesday are capitalized but summer is not.

Directions

You capitalize the names of places and regions of the country but not the cardinal directions.

This one is confusing because west is a direction and a region of the country. So is south. So you have to pay attention to how the word is used.

> How the West was won. (region of the country)
> Go west, young man. (direction)

Titles

Capitalize titles when they are used as part of a person's name but not when they are used alone. In this case, titles are things like doctor, lady, duke, military rank, or officer.

> The doctor is in.

CAPITALIZATION

You will see Doctor Adams.

The exception to this is very important people. And I mean very selectively important people. The President is capitalized even when it is not followed by a name, but only when you are talking about the President of the United States. If you are talking about the president of the student body, lower case.

There are different rules for capitalizing titles, but we covered that in Chapter 16, Titles.

Subjects

The names of subjects that you study in school are only capitalized if they are languages.

I took geometry and English.

But if it is the name of a specific course, it is capitalized.

I took Intro to Geometry.

In capitalization, *consistency* matters most. Why do we have these rules? The rules create consistency. But let's say you are writing an essay and you want to distinguish between something that is true and universal truths. You can capitalize "Truth" to represent universal truths, so long as you do it the same way throughout the entire essay. If you flip back and forth, you have made a worse capitalization error than any other kind, because now you have made things confusing.

You will have some professors who won't allow you this leeway, but in the real world, we can use capitalization to distinguish the way we use terms, for emphasis, and for rhetorical effect, as long as we do it consistently.

Consistency is key!

Our goal is always to be clear, and consistency leads to clarity. Why do we have all these rules? So that we will all be consistent.

If you do something one way, do it that way for your whole essay.

Want more on this? Go to madskillzacademics.com.

Capitalization
EXERCISES

Each paragraph has five errors. Find and correct them. They could be anything we have covered so far.

1.

The Civil War was a transitional war from inaccurate weapons to deadly weapons that led to massive casualties. During the course of the war Navies went from wooden boats to iron plated war ships, there were even rudimentary submarines in use. Ships moved South to blockade the ports of the South. While the first massive bombings led to the first instances of trench warfare. To this day, Americans have never suffered more casualties than they did during the Civil War.

2.

The Winter is considered "the Holiday Season," but other seasons also have holidays. During the Summer we have the fourth of July. Who doesn't like fireworks and hotdogs. That person isn't an American. Spring is time for Easter. There are reasons to celebrate during every part of the year.

3.

Several cities have been built around a main river or body of water, like Columbus, Ohio, Chicago, Illinois, and Portland, Oregon. This is due to the fact that rivers used to be a primary mode of transportation. Building beside a river gave the City access to trade and travel. The Missouri river was like a super highway. Today, we use Freeways to do this same thing but these old cities aren't likely to get up and move.

4.

The tallest building in the world is in Dubai. Its one of the strange features of humanity that people are willing to spend millions of

CAPITALIZATION

dollars to get that title. Many tall buildings, like the empire state building, is topped with spires to increase the height. Tall buildings offer a few benefits, they increase the usage of a small piece of land and help decrease urban sprawl. However it seems the primary motivation in building them is to be a part of an International spitting contest.

5.

My family went to visit a monastery. My Brother met a monk, and said "how are you, Brother?" The monk gave my Mom a jar of honey. We loved walking around the Garden. It was designed to be a replica of the Garden of Gethsemane. I recommend a visit.

6.

The vitamin string quartet are a group of classical musicians who play modern music. A traditional quartet is made of four musicians. Usually two violins, a viola, and a cello. These are not the typical instruments of pop music. The group takes a song like Don't stop Believing and creates a new arrangement suited to a quartet. Its very interesting to listen to, but it does lead one to the realization that most pop music is simple and repetitive. To hear something pleasingly complex, one must turn to real classical music.

7.

Wearing crazy, creative costumes, and eating tons of candy are the best parts of Halloween. Other holidays would be more fun, if they followed Halloweens lead. If everyone at thanksgiving dinner dressed like zombies, they would enjoy it more. Easter already has candy, but what if we all shouted "Trick or treat!" at the Easter bunny?

REMEMBER:
Names are capitalized.

The answers to these exercises are in the back of this book.

89

HYPHENS

This is a hyphen -. It is a short line. This is a dash—. It is longer than a hyphen. Your keyboard does not have a dash key. Dashes are made by typing a hyphen twice and putting at least one letter after. This will cause your word processor to make a dash. There are actually two kinds of dashes, an m dash and an n dash, but we aren't going to worry about that. If you really like dashes, you can go learn more. For now, we are going to talk about hyphens.

Hyphens and dashes may look similar, but they are used in dramatically different ways. Hyphens are used to connect words.

There are some phrases that always get hyphens.

Mother-in-law
jack-of-all-trades
Post-industrial

There are some prefixes that get hyphens.

all-encompassing
self-doubt
Ex-husband

And when fractions and certain numbers are written out, they get a hyphen.

Thirty-two
One-fourth

The good news is that these uses of hyphens are in the dictionary and your spell check will usually find them for you. Still, it is important to be smarter than your computer to prevent Skynet from taking over. You've seen *The Terminator*. The lesson of that movie is that you should learn grammar so that the computers don't develop time travel.

One of the ways language changes and grows is that people start putting together words so often that they become one new word. At any given time, you are living with words that long ago became one word (goodbye, waterproof), words that are well on their way to being one word (baby-proof) and words that are just starting to be grouped together often (ground zero, baby daddy). Hyphens are part of this process, and because it is a process, there are lots of phrases that have an optional hyphen. This makes hyphen use seem confusing and arbitrary.

Hyphens are used to connect words.

self-
ex-
-elect
fractions
forty-eight

Not sure if a phrase gets a hyphen? Look it up.

merriam-webster.com

HYPHENS

There is a logic behind the madness. There is. As language changes, it takes time for the writing to catch up.

The other reason to connect words is when two or more words are making one modifier. If I say

I want to bring my short, adorable dog.

then "dog" has two modifiers. The dog is short and the dog is adorable. When I have two or more modifiers like this, I put a comma between them. If you can replace the comma with the word "and" and the sentence makes the same sense, you are punctuating correctly.

However, if I say

I want to bring my brand new dog.

then dog has one modifier. If I said "my brand and new dog," no one would understand me. What is a brand dog? It's nothing. So I have two words working as one modifier. This is when I want to make sure people read this correctly by using a hyphen.

I want to bring my brand-new dog.

This does not work when one of the modifiers ends in –ly. And this *only* works when the modifiers are on top of the word they are modifying. If I wrote

My dog is brand new.

then definitely don't use a hyphen.

This is one of those things that you can see people use irregularly. Even in professional writing, the hyphen sometimes comes and goes. That's why getting the hang of the hyphen is so fun. It does help the reader understand you slightly faster, and it makes you seem masterful.

Two or more words working as one modifier get a hyphen.
(if the modifier is before what it is modifying and not including adverbs)

Want more on this? Go to madskillzacademics.com.

HYPHENS

Each paragraph has five errors. Find and correct them. They could be anything we have covered so far.

1.

Shopping at thrift stores, and finding cool-fashionable clothes to where is a skill that not everyone has, some people can only see rack after rack of old clothes. My sister in law is one of the people who can shop at a thrift store. She is self aware enough that she knows what works for her.

2.

Our culture tends to celebrate cool people; people who pass through life unruffled and untouched by the things of the world or the person who can walk away calmly while the building explodes behind them. I don't believe we should celebrate the detached person with a devil may care attitude. We should celebrate messy, passionate people. We should be messy and passionate. We should dive deep into life instead of trying to rise above it. Rumi wrote Sell your cleverness and buy bewilderment." Life is bewildering and that is what makes it overwhelming, heartbreaking, and wonderful.

3.

When a person is in an apple pie eating mood, they will come up against a tremendous choice. Because their are three kinds of apple pies. The dutch apple pie is the one that is topped with crumbles instead of crust. Lattice is where strips of pie crust are laid over the top of the pie in a checkerboard pattern. The last kind has a crust lid over the top of the pie. Trying to analyze which of these styles of pies is the best is nearly impossible; they are all fabulously delicious.

4.

Dogs are loyal, selfless animals that human-kind has used in a

HYPHENS

hundred different ways. Because of all the service that dogs do people ought to take care of dogs when they are old and sick. However, people do not have a great track record in that area. In certain large apartment complexes, people will leave their dog loose in the complex when they move. People will take older dogs to the shelter, and leave them there, these people cannot imagine a dogs' inner life. Fortunately, many good people work hard to save these abandoned animals.

5.

Have you ever had a happy go lucky day? Have you had a get rich quick day or a garbage day. I prefer to have family-and-friends days, or dance to the music in the car days.

6.

My dog has a little Wonder-Woman costume that my Mom gave her. It is to small for her and has a stupid looking skirt. My dog loves it. She gets nervous at night, and is only able to calm down when she wears it. She has many other toys, blankets, and pillows, but none of them work as well as the costume does.

7.

My friend Daniel is at a crossroads in his life and I want to support him as he makes tough decisions. Daniel's ex boyfriend brought him babys-breath in a half hearted attempt to win Daniel back. Daniel refused the flower, though, because post-breakup, he has discovered that he needs more alone time. Also, why should he invest all of his heart in someone who is only lukewarm.

Are you confused by any of these exercises or by the answers? There is a forum at madskillzacademics.com where you can ask questions.

The answers to these exercises are in the back of this book.

NUMBERS

This is the last topic we are going to cover in this book. We have not covered everything there is to know about proofreading, but if you master what we have covered, then you will be able to avoid 95% of the errors I routinely see in student writing.

This is a tough one. The way I summarize numbers with my students is this:

Look it up. Every single time. Look it up.

The reason that numbers are so hard is that the rules change if you are using MLA, APA, or the Chicago Manual of Style. If you are not yet familiar with these terms, they are collections of rules set forth by different organizations to create consistency within a certain discipline. MLA is used by the humanities, and when you are writing about language or literature, you don't use many numbers. APA is for the sciences where people are constantly using numbers and statistical analysis. The rules you will follow will depend on your major or the field of study you are working in.

The rules change based on what is being numbered. They can change again if you are numbering two things in one sentence.

Here's what you need to remember: the rules about numbers are designed to make them as easy to read as possible. A number like 978,631 is easier to read as digits than written out as nine hundred and seventy eight thousand, six hundred and thirty one. But one million is easier to read than 1,000,000. This is the MLA approach.

Over in the sciences, where numbers show up all the time, the general rule is digits for everything except one through nine.

Are you confused yet? Don't be. Know what style guide your class is using, and look it up.

Here are a few things that are almost always true.

If a number is the first word in a sentence, ignore everything else and write it out.

If within a sentence you use numbers for multiple things, combine digits and words to minimize confusion:

100 eighteen wheelers
a thousand 10 cent pieces

See how the numbers are back to back, so all digits would be confusing to read?

Be consistent. If you use digits when you are writing the number of cars, use digits for every time you number cars. Even if the "rules" would say to use words, stick with the way the first number of

rule 1: Look it up!
rule 2: Don't start a sentence with digits.
rule 3: Make your numbers clear and easy to read.
rule 4: Use digits for dates, times, exact amounts of money, and parts of a play.
rule 5: look it up!

NUMBERS

cars was presented.

I have one car, but the dealership has a thousand cars.

And look it up!
You should have bought some kind of reference guide for your English class. You will know it as the book you probably didn't have any homework in. This is a precious tool. I keep one beside my computer at all times. It is only good for one thing, but that one thing is pretty huge. It's where I look it up.

I need my brain for better things than memorizing MLA. I look it up.

You will use digits when writing dates, times, percentages, exact amounts of money, sports scores, addresses, and parts of a play. Because we don't know what style guide you are using, we are going to only focus on following the general rules. But every time you see a number, I want you to say, "Look it up!"

Want more on this? Go to madskillzacademics.com.

NUMBERS

Each paragraph has five errors. Find and correct them. They could be anything we have covered so far.

1.

I currently live in Southern California. Which is half-great weather and half douche-bag people. It doesn't get very cold in the winter. 200 days out of the year are clear and sunny; maybe more. The tradeoff is that southern Californians are not friendly people. Driving on the freeways feels like competing in a death-match. I met a woman who had lived here her whole life and had worked in the film industry. When she was diagnosed with cancer all of her friends disappeared.

2.

Their is a student loan crisis in America: Students are taking out massive loans to enter low paying fields. I have a friend who borrowed one hundred thousand two hundred and sixty seven dollars to get a degree in social work. A career where the average salary is 40 thousand dollars a year. This is bad math. The solution to the student loan crisis is to better educate students about the consequences of these massive loans. To keep students from taking them out to begin with.

3.

Imagine a city with five farms. Two farms are next too each other. If 4 farms grow 100 pounds of food a year, how many farms does it take to grow a thousand pounds? I am just kidding. This looks like a word problem but I just needed a reason to write numbers, and their aren't many situations in academic writing where numbers come up.

NUMBERS

Except in the sciences.

4.

Everyone should be able to cook. Eating out or eating frozen food all the time are expensive unhealthy and unwise. Making a salad at home costs four dollars and fifty cents in ingredients but the same salad in a restaurant would cost 10. A value meal from a hamburger drive through can be around 2000 calories, that is the number of calories a person should eat all day. In addition, a value meal will be high in fat, sodium, and sugar. Making a meal at home gives the cook control over the amount of salt added, and while beans and rice are not as delicious as hamburgers, that meal will be four hundred calories and high in fiber.

5.

Its not unique to say this, but I hate colds. For me, colds follow the same pattern every time. On the 1st day, I may feel a tickle in my throat, and I know than that I better start fighting it off. After 2 or three days comes the great sleep- that is when I take to my bed. After a good sleep, I always think I am better before I actually am. I have a lot to do; I hate being trapped in bed. Then I get sicker. Ultimately, I recover, but the whole process takes anywhere from four to seven days. All of them miserable.

6.

When the founding fathers began planning the new country they intended to make in the seventeen hundreds, they were worried about tyranny. Having just escaped a king through war, they did not want the country to fall under the influence of a king again. However the people in the former colonies were not so dead set. The people thought they had had a bad king, now they would get a good king. The people wanted to make George Washington king. He declined. He understood that having a king at all meant eventually having a bad king. No one in history had every escaped that. Now in twenty eighteen, many people have lost their fear of tyranny. Many people would be fine with a king that agreed with them politically because they don't understand that giving up the power of the people to a king cannot be reversed when the king doesn't agree with them anymore.

7.

There is one special time of every year, when people leave thier families behind in order to go out into the world and be terrible. The time is called black Friday. Do you need 7 5 dollar toasters more than you need human decency. Than save all your aggression for this one special day. If you aren't bleeding, you aren't doing it right.

The answers to these exercises are in the back of this book.

TEST YOURSELF

Humans: cheating Biology

The idea of the existence of apex predators are that certain animals are at the top of the food chain, although everything is eaten by something else. In the case of an apex species like a grizzly bear or a lion there is no larger animal that they have to fear. Nothing hunts tigers. We consider humans to be apex predators to but this is an act of vanity, not science.

Our place at the top of the food chain is unnatural. We think of ourselves as the equals of bears and lions but this is laughably untrue. We are hairless apes. Slow, vulnerable, weak, and very tasty. Our ancestors were constantly being eaten by actual apex predators; they grouped into tribes, because they were incapable of surviving long alone.

In fact, many of the characteristics we have as human beings comes from having been pray. Our hands are good for climbing trees to hide, our eyes are well-developed to see colors in order to spot predators. We walk on two legs to get a better view of our surroundings, and spot predators while they are far away. Our teeth are mostly good for ripping the leaves off of twigs and grinding those leaves up enough to swallow. Do we have claws. No, we have fingernails, they are good for prying into ant hills, and not for tearing open arteries.

Do bears lift their heads? Are they twitchy and nervous like prey animals? No. While rabbits and dear must be

Now let's put what you've learned to work. This test has approximately fifty errors. You may count differently than I did, but it doesn't matter. Find and correct everything you can.

The answers to this test are available to you, along with a video explanation, at madskillzacademics.com.

This is about you measuring your own progress. This test will show you where your weaknesses are. Whatever you struggle with here, you have a chance to review and improve upon.

TEST YOURSELF

constantly alert an apex predator can relax. Nothing is coming to eat them. Humans struggle to relax. We have to take medication to calm our anxieties, because our nervousness is hardwired into our biology from all the times our ancestors were eaten.

Take the strongest, fastest, most ruthless human being and pit that human being against any apex predator. Oh take away all the trappings human beings have used to cheat nature. Take away guns and knives. Take away clothes and shoes. They're is no apex predator that a human being could beat in hand to hand combat; lion, tiger, polar bear, orca, panther, or salt water crocodile. A true predator wouldn't even break a sweat taking out a person.

Honestly a naked human being could be killed by a deer or a moose. In fact, the list would be shorter, if we only mentioned the animals that couldn't kill us.

The thing that changed humans from midday snacks to top carnivores were not people. People didn't get better at anything. It was dogs. Wolves are also not apex predators. They are cooperative hunters and when the first canines were domesticated, they began hunting cooperatively with people. This was a deadly combination; the first example of synergy. People are slow, but the way we are built makes us able to walk long distances. This is not good for hunting but it is good for scavenging. Dogs do have speed. They have sharp teeth and powerful jaws. They have an amazing sense of smell, and can track large prey and take it down. In fact, the real question is what did humans offer in this equation. Human intelligence is the standard answer, and boy do we like to think of ourselves as hunting masterminds.

Actually the advantage of human intelligence was food preservation. Every other predator gets a big kill, and eats until they are bursting, and then they starve for 2 weeks until the next big kill. Humans were not designed to be great predators. At best, we were opportunistic carnivores. If something small enough stumbled into our path we'd eat it. Their is archeological proof that the Anasazi people living near the Great Salt Lake survived on crickets

100

that would die around the lake. Bugs were things humans could regularly catch, and eat.

Human beings could not benefit from a large kill. Not only were they not equipped to kill something big. They couldn't eat much even if they did. We are designed to graze; we eat multiple times a day, and if there's a bowl of candies nearby, we can eat continuously for hours. While real predators were gorging themselves and moving on, a human figured out jerky. If they dried out the meat using the sun it would last longer, and they could carry it with them. Suddenly, big kills meant a month of food. Not only did this bring humans more into the meat-eating game but it gave dogs a reason to stick around. Why spend most of your time starving when you could team up with this tall, soft-monkey thing, and eat regularly, or as regularly as anything could eat in those days, and not have to worry about the next big kill as much.

Dogs transformed people from a mediocre hunter that lived mostly on gathering into a new apex predator. That may be why hunting is so thrilling to people still. It is not natural to us. Imagine how an ibex would feel if it could turn around, and blow away a cheetah. That ibex would definitely want it's picture taken with the dead cheetah and would post about it on ibex Facebook. Compare that to how the cheetah feels about killing an ibex. The cheetah says no big deal. This is what I do.

A certain variety of insecure man feels that killing a bear makes him more manly. He does so with a gun that he did not invent; usually led by paid guides, because this same man can't find his way through the woods alone. Trophy hunting proves how weak a man is, not how strong. It proves how much they rely on the inventions of smarter people and therefore how helpless humans would be without them.

So the next time nothing eats you, thank a dog. Without dogs, our species would never have started down the path that has brought us airplanes and pumpkin spice lattes. Without dogs, people would still be on the menu for other bigger, stronger animals.

Stop. Don't move on to this test until you have reviewed the things you had difficulty with on Test 1. There are multiple tests so that you can make multiple attempts to absorb this material.

This test has approximately fifty errors. You may count differently than I did, but it doesn't matter. Find and correct everything you can.

The answers to this test are available to you, along with a video explanation, at madskillzacademics.com.

TEST YOURSELF

We have made it to the end of the semester. Your probably worrying about the finals you have to take, and planning what your going to do with your vacation time.

Education is not a linear path, its a wandering journey where you pick something up here, and another thing their. It's like walking along a long beach and collecting a shell and a piece of driftwood and one day you look back and discover you were making something without ever realizing it.

There are classes you take, and forget everything you learned, I once knew how to do calculus. I don't regret taking that class, because I had the strangest professor. He was a tall, thin, grumpy man who like to go cross country skiing. He came to class once dressed in knickers, and a wool vest. When he skied he dressed like a newspaper boy from the 1920's.

I was in that class with a good friend. We named our book George, and when we wanted to check our answers in the back of the book, we would say that, "we were going to ask George."

Of all my many different college experiences the most important happened outside of class. I read a book called "Life and the Art Of Motorcycle maintenance" that opened my brain up to a new way of thinking. Then I read A Pilgrim at Tinker Creek. Annie Dillards way of seeing things changed how I saw things. That book which I read as a freshman won the pulitzer prize.

Reading opens up new worlds, books are better than

TEST YOURSELF

movies.

Your life will be full of choices; but the most important one will be if you choose to pay attention. Or if you choose to sleepwalk. You will find that life has a way of wearing you down. You might have children or you might end up taking care of a sick parent. Sometimes you will feel like they're is to much to do. Dang it is easy to be overwhelmed.

You can learn from anything, so be sure to find the lesson. When bad things happen. You can let them knock you down or you can find a way to become stronger. If the plans you make fall apart, you make new plans. It isn't easy, because the world can be brutal. Every day is a matter of life and death but to many people forget that.

When 1 door closes. Climb in a window. Weather you work in a bank or work cleaning the bank, you're life is valuable. A man who lost all control of his body wrote a book by blinking, think of what you are capable of. If you lose everything you will never lose your education. If you have no money you still have your mind, and your imagination. Like the rolling stones song says. You can't always get what you want, but if you try sometimes you get what you need.

Love freely and with generosity. If you love 5 or 6 people you are rich.

Remember Ebenezer scrooge from a Christmas carol. When he was young he was in love but he kept putting off the wedding until his girlfriend moved on. He thought it was important to be established in business but his priorities were all wrong. It took three Ghosts visiting him, to make him realize he had wasted his life. He was stingy with money but more important he was stingy, with his love. In the end, he is happy, because he loves Tiny Tim. You should watch "A Christmas Carol" again; if you haven't seen it lately. It's great.

I hope you all go on to great success; and I hope you remember how to write an essay. I hope you read more, and love more. I hope you live great lives, and I hope you find happiness.

Stop. Don't move on to this test until you have reviewed the things you had difficulty with on Test 2. There are multiple tests so that you can make multiple attempts to absorb this material.

This test has approximately fifty errors. You may count differently than I did, but it doesn't matter. Find and correct everything you can.

The answers to this test are available to you, along with a video explanation, at madskillzacademics.com.

TEST YOURSELF
An ode to Winter

Every season of the year has it's benefits. Summer is hot and unrelenting but all that sunshine and heat grows food. Spring is a series of small miracles, one day is gloomy and wet, and the next, all the flowers have bloomed. During Fall in New England the trees put on all their brightest colors. People travel from 100s of miles to see the leaves change. There is a chill in the air and you can smell people burning wood fires.

But winter is the best of all.

For one thing, star gazing is the best during a clear winter night. The cold air pulls the moisture from the air and every star is a sharp prick of light in the deepness of a dark sky. If you are lucky enough to escape the glare of the city lights, and you have a thermos full of hot chocolate, you can lean back on the hood of your car and see. Millions of stars, stars on top of stars. They take your breath away. The purple band of stars that arcs overhead are the Milky Way Galaxy, the Galaxy we are just a small part of. If you ever lose your sense of wonder their is one place you can always find it again in the stars.

Another wonderful part of winter is how the cold and the darkness makes people stay inside. During the rest of the year you are so busy going so many places. But winters cold whether makes those going out plans not quite as appealing as they once were. Where a couple in the summer might have headed to dinner and a movie, winter convinces them to stay in. Watch a DVD, cuddle on the couch under a cozy blanket. Oh winter nights are no time for heaters!

Winter food is also terrific, winter is when you can eat whatever you want, because a sweater will cover up any extra pounds. Its the time of the year for eating crusty bread with piles of butter, hot-spicy soups, and fresh from the oven cookies. If you bake you know how an oven can overheat an apartment in the summer. However that isn't a problem in winter. Summer and fall may have fresh vegetables but how do you eat them. Fresh vegetables mean salads, winter vegetables are potatoes.

As I once said about potatoes. I love them!

When I lived in Chicago, the lake would freeze. The waves would be caught in mid crash and kept there. As spray hit the pilings, the drops would freeze, and they would pile up into strange, beautiful sculptures along the lake side. They were a gift to the people riding the bus into the city for work, as though the lake was rewarding us for getting out in the cold. When I was young, an ice storm passed thru my home town. Overnight, every tree was coated in a perfect layer of ice. The whole world was remade in diamonds and when the sun came out every part of the world sparkled. The weight of the ice pulled some of the more slender trees over, and even though the ice melted away a week later, there was a permanent bend in it's trunk.

Winter is a time to slow down, it is a time to appreciate loved ones. Summer is a time to be outside and winter is time to be inside. As it says in Ecclesiastes chapter three verse one To everything there is a season, and a time to every purpose under the heaven." Winter is a time for hiding, for hibernating, for burrowing, and for patience. Which we don't have enough of in our fast paced, modern life. The Byrds made that bible verse into a song that is known by the title Turn Turn Turn. It means, let the seasons of life turn, don't resist time, because every phase of life has meaning.

So much technology was invented to protect us from the world. That is mostly a very good thing. Winter no longer means starvation too most of us. It no longer means isolation or danger but we should not let that mean that winter means nothing at all. Winter is beautiful, and every day that we are alive is a gift to be appreciated.

If you are having trouble finding errors, start at the end, and read one sentence at a time until you get to the beginning. Professional proofreaders do this to keep their minds from skipping over errors.

TEST YOURSELF

THE EVIL WITHIN

Roughly fifteen percent of the human population are born with a strange and frightening defect. When this defect manifests itself it must be stamped out immediately. Beat the child, if you must. Don't let anyone be left handed, this is the attitude people had towards lefties for thousands of years.

For a very long time the left-hand was associated with the devil. In the Bible, God's right hand was symbolically the place for good and the left hand was the side for evil. In Medieval Europe, religion was a powerful force and education was not. Most people were illiterate, and knew very little of the world, so they tended to dwell heavily on what little they did know. They took the Bible literally, and hurt people because of it.

In fact, the word sinister, comes from Latin for "on the left hand or side." The word "left" comes from the word for weak and western culture is not alone in this type of discrimination. Middle Eastern and Asian cultures also look down on lefties.

So what happened to children born left handed. They would be forced to be right-handed. As late as the seventies, teachers would encourage left-handed students to switch hands. When they were learning to write. They would often encourage them by smacking their left hands every time they tried to use them.

My father is a southpaw. He had a teacher tie his left

Stop. Don't move on to this test until you have reviewed the things you had difficulty with on Test 3. There are multiple tests so that you can make multiple attempts to absorb this material.

This test has approximately fifty errors. You may count differently than I did, but it doesn't matter. Find and correct everything you can.

The answers to this test are available to you, along with a video explanation, at madskillzacademics.com.

hand behind his back to force him to write with his right hand. He tried to do what people wanted but when he was in high school, he gave up and went back to using his left hand. To this day, he has terrible hand writing. He didn't practice his penmanship with his left enough when he was younger; but he feels much better about it.

That may not seem like a big deal but if you have ever tried to do something with your non-dominant hand, you understand. The dominant hand is not an accident; its hard wired into the structures of the brain.

"Oh" a person might say, "Lefties used to be persecuted but today everything is different, everything is completely fair."

"Oh, no says the leftie. "Their are still lots of ways my life is made harder. Because our writing travels from left to right I end up rubbing my hand over what I just wrote. This smudges the ink, or gets my hand dirty. You can see the last few words written; I cannot."

"That's not so bad" the person says. The leftie than says, "Cars have the stick shift available to the right hand. Scissors and can openers are made for righties, I have to purchase special scissors. Most of the classroom desks where the table top is attached to the chair is made for you. There are special desks made for left handers but they can be difficult to find. Even credit card swipe machines are made for people to use right handed.

Twenty two percent of pitchers in professional baseball are left-handed. This is because batters face left handers less often so left handed pitchers have a built in advantage.

President Obama is the 7th president to be a leftie, that we know of. There may have been more but of course, most of our presidents lived in times when a child writing with his or her left hand would have gotten them smacked with a ruler too break that nasty habit. He is the forty fourth president. That puts the number of left handed presidents slightly ahead statistically of the general population.

TEST YOURSELF

Because all of this comes down to how the brain is constructed; there are people who are truly ambidextrous. That means they don't have a dominant hand; they can use either one equally well. Which probably means that they have brains that are more thoroughly constructed. In addition, deliberately writing with your non dominant hand is a good mental exercise. Musicians who learn to use both hands equally well show actual brain growth. Specifically, where the hemispheres of the brain connect. This means that they have made it possible for the sides of the brain to communicate more effectively. While we don't know for sure what that might mean, we know that it is good to have a more developed brain.

Looking back at history, it seems the hand a person uses is one more example of how ignorance has led to unkindness. Being left handed is perfectly normal and acceptable, and hopefully every left hander knows this.

Stop. This is the last test. Don't move on to this test until you have reviewed the things you had difficulty with on Test 4. There are multiple tests so that you can make multiple attempts to absorb this material.

This test has approximately fifty errors. You may count differently than I did, but it doesn't matter. Find and correct everything you can.

The answers to this test are available to you, along with a video explanation, at madskillzacademics.com.

TEST YOURSELF

Monsters come from People

Monsters are a fundamentally human invention; they exist in legends from the entire world and throughout all recorded history. Why are monsters so popular. Many monsters express the fears and obsessions of the culture they arise from. In western culture, the most popular and long lived monster lore arises from the fear of death, the fear of wildness, and the fear of technology.

The fear of death is straightforward. For that, we can look at vampires. The Vampire legends arose in eastern Europe, and spread at a time when the Christian church was strong. In the meantime superstition and paganism were equally strong. While the Christian tradition presented ideas of resurrection and afterlife fears of witchcraft and the unknown mingled with it, and created a fear that dead people would come back to life to wreak havoc on the living. People would reopen caskets and see signs and changes in the body that we now know to be completely normal; but the people at the time saw it as evidence that this person was not fully dead.

The symbolism of blood, and the vampires drinking blood is a particularly Christian symbol. The consumption of Christ's blood in church ritual crossed into the legend of vampire. Not only did vampires become the embodiment of the fear of death. They also absorbed Christian symbols in that fear.

Imagine that a loved one had died, and you saw signs

that they might still be living. I would expect most people would be overjoyed instead of horrified. Lacking an understanding of nature the people at the time attributed every bad thing that happened in the village to the night time wanderings of the dead. So they would put a stake through the heart of the suspected corpse.

At the time, expected life spans were shorter, death was a regular part of life. Bodies would be prepared for burial by family members, and laid out on dining room tables. All the same death was a fearful thing.

Another aspect of the vampire is it's sexuality. In early vampire lore, the vampire did things like make farm animals die, cause crops to wither, or give someone warts. Anything that the people couldn't explain logically. When Bram Stoker wrote "Dracula", the bad things the vampire did changed to murder and seducing innocent young women. By the time Dracula was written, failing crops were understood, and the anxiety of society had moved into a fear of women misbehaving. Heaven forbid a young lady have desires.

The vampire endured as a monster, because the mystery and fear around death persisted, and possibly intensified. What was mingled with death changed from a fear of a harsh and unpredictable natural world to a fear of unrestrained sexuality. In the nineties, with Anne Rices book "Interview With a Vampire," the sexuality to fear was gay sexuality and other types of "fringe" sexual expression. Next, it will be something different.

The fear of wildness is seen in the form of the werewolf, a werewolf is a person who has within them something primitive and impossible to control. This correlates neatly with how all people experience society. Their are desires and urges we all have but we control them in order to function together. When my neighbor is noisy late at night my impulse might be to attack them with a knife but I do not do this because society has created consequences. Because my desire to be a part of society is greater than my desire for revenge on my horrible neighbor.

However we all know of examples where people have made the opposite decision. When that happens too often, society begins to crumble. Though we are all capable of savage actions we restrain ourselves as part of the social contract. If we didn't no one could ride on a bus, or eat at a restaurant without being attacked. The werewolf is the manifestation of that dichotomy, in one person is both the civilized individual and the animal.

Finally, there is the fear of technology. Represented by newer monsters, or old monsters reinvented. Technology as a potential menace is fairly new too society but not so new as one might think. We see this in the story of Frankenstein's monster Mary Shelley wrote Frankenstein in the year eighteen eighteen. More recently, there have been killer robots and alien invasions, the zombie has been remade into the product of science, often being the result of a scientifically created virus. Still Frankenstein's monster is the prototypical monster arising from the fear of technology.

Frankenstein's monster was made by Dr. Frankenstein, the first of many scientists in horror to fail to consider what he should do, being consumed only with what he could do.

In the original book, Frankenstein's monster is brought into a world where he is despised. The horrors of life are heaped upon his head but in subsequent retellings, the monster becomes a menace to people. This is a fascinating flip. In Mary Shelley's time, the fear was for what would become of what we made. That was before nuclear weapons or cars were invented. Today, we fear what the thing made will do to us.

Zombies are an extension of the Frankenstein monster. They are most often man made, mindless killers, horrifying because they are contagious and there sheer numbers. The old fear of the vivisectionist became mingled with the fear of Science and epidemics. It makes sense, as advances in travel have made epidemics harder to contain and potentially devastating.

In short, looking closely at the monsters of a society gives us a glimpse of that societys' fearful obsessions. Although they have change over time. It also explains why monsters must be routinely reinvented in order to maintain their potency.

Our goal is not perfection. Perfection is impossible. Our goal is always improvement.

If you have improved your proofreading skills, congratulations.

You did it!

ALL THE ANSWERS
CHAPTER 2

noun-n   verb-v   modifier-m   conjunction-con

article-art   interjection-int   preposition-pr

1

```
    pr  art  n  con    pr   art  n    pr    m           n   n   v
```
1. Over the river and through the woods, to grandmother's house we go.
```
   n   v  art    n       v  pr art n  con   m    n     v    m    con   m       con
```
2. I want the opportunity to be in a class where my classmates are excellent and admirable, and
```
art   n   v   v    pr   m    n
```
the teacher is teaching to that level.
```
      n   v   v   art   n   con  n    v   n
```
3. They are facing the abyss and they know it.
```
  int   n   n   v    art m   n  pr   n
```
4. Crap, John, we missed the last train to Frankfurter!
```
   n   v   n    con      n    v   v    n
```
5. You wear armor so that nothing will touch you.
```
  n   v m   v     m
```
6. I can't get enough.

> "Can't" is a contraction of "can" and "not." "Can" is a verb. "Not" is an adverb, a type of modifier.

```
   pr art  n  pr art    n       m   m    n      v  v  v  pr art    m       n
```
7. In the event of an accident, your seat cushion can be used as a floatation device.
```
   con   n   pr art   n      v   m    v   con   n    v   n        m
```
8. But those with the courage to go forward discover that there is something more.
```
      n      v   v   v   m   n    con  n   v  art   n    m   m    n
```
9. Carol Burnett seemed to be having so much fun, and she gave the audience so much joy.
```
     con  n   v  art    m    n   n  v  v  con  v  pr m  n
```
10. When she was the cleaning lady, she'd stop and lean on her mop.

> Gerund phrase! We cover this in the next chapter.

PRACTICE TWO

```
   pr  n   n  v    m    n  pr   n    pr  n    v    n   con   v
```
1. In total, I have seven years of experience in karate, taking classes and fighting.
```
   n    v  art m    n  con art   n     v     v   con  n   v   v
```
2. There was a rapt silence as the audience waited to see what she would do.
```
    v    pr   n  pr  n  v  v    m   con art  n    v   v    n   pr art n
```
3. Getting from place to place can be difficult when a person has lost access to a car.
```
   con   v   n  v   v   art    n    m  pr art    m      n     v   art   n
```
4. When do we have to get the diamond back to the enchanted temple to break the spell?
```
  con art   n     v    n   v   m     n   m   m   n  con  v   m    v    m
```
5. As the preacher speaks, Sarah grips Henry's hand one last time and bends over to kiss his
```
   n
```
forehead.
```
     v    pr art   n  pr art  n  n v  v     art   n  v   m
```
6. Sitting on the dock of the bay, I'm watching the tide roll away.
```
   n    v m  v   art   n
```
7. You can't handle the truth!
```
   n   v  art   n   con  m  m   m      n      v   m  n   v pr art   n      con    n   v  m v
```
8. I have a dream that my four little children will one day live in a nation where they will not be
```

114
```

ALL THE ANSWERS chapter 2

 v   pr art   n   pr m   n con pr art   n   pr m   n
judged by the color of their skin but by the content of their character.
   con   n   v   art n con   n   v   pr n art m   n   con art m
9. However, Jose preferred the offer that Yale made to him: a full-ride scholarship and a lifetime
 n   pr m   m   n
supply of oatmeal cream pies.
    v   n   pr m m   n
10. Say "hello" to my little friend!

PRACTICE THREE
   m   n   v   n   art   m   n pr art n pr art n
1. Today, I consider myself the luckiest man on the face of the earth.
   m   n   n   v pr m n   n   n v m
2. Trappist Monk Thomas Merton wrote in his book, *Contemplative Prayer,* "I cannot
   v   m   n   con n v   v   art   n   con   v   pr m   v   m
discover my 'meaning' if I try to evade the dread which comes from first experiencing my
     n
meaninglessness!"
  int   v   v   n v pr art   m   m   n   con m   m   n   v pr art   m   m
3. Oh, say, can you see by the dawn's early light what so proudly we hailed at the twilight's last
    n   ┌─────────────────────────────────────┐
gleaming?   │ Another gerund. We'll see in the next chapter, │
              │ it looks like a verb but acts like a noun. │
              └─────────────────────────────────────┘
  pr n   v   art m   n   art   m   n   v   v   v   v
4. In order to survive a zombie apocalypse, a resourceful person needs to be willing to sacrifice
  m   n con m   n
any friend or family member.
  n   v   m   n pr m   n   v   m   m
5. We are not here on this earth to pass through undamaged.
  int   v   m
6. Hey! Watch out!
  n v   m con n con n v   m   v   v   n   m
7. I'm mad as hell, and I'm not going to take it anymore!
   n   v   v n con art n   v   m pr art   n   v   con v   pr m
8. You can see it when a team runs out on the field, whooping and dancing with slightly
   m   n
strained smiles.
   int   n
9. Damn, Daniel!
      v   m   n   con n v pr n
10. Curse these shackles that you put on me.

PRACTICE FOUR
  n   v   m   n   v   m   con m n   v   v   n   con n v
1. We hold these truths to be self-evident, that all men are created equal, that they are
   v   pr m   n   pr m   m   n   con   m   n   v   n   n
endowed by their creator with certain unalienable Rights, that among these are Life, Liberty,
con art   n   pr n
and the pursuit of Happiness.

115

int m   n   m   m   n v m m   n
2. Oh my gosh, this tank top is only ten bucks!

We can treat the whole phrase "Oh my gosh" as an interjection. It mean nothing. It expresses emotion.

art   n   v   m   pr art   v   pr art   n   v   m   pr art
3. The undersigned, known forthwith as the renter, agrees to the terms set forth by the

n   pr m   n
landlord in this contract.

m   n v   v   m   n   con   v   n pr n art   m   m
4. Someday, I hope to shake Martha Stewart's hand and thank her for all the amazing cookie

n
recipes.

n   n v art n   n v m pr   n   m
5. Toto, I've a feeling we're not in Kansas anymore.

n   v   con n v art   m   n   con n v   m   m   n   pr   m
6. I know that this is a controversial stance, but I prefer oatmeal raisin cookies to chocolate

n   m   pr   n   con n v m   v   art   n pr art   n
chip, especially in situations where I don't know the baker of the cookies.

n   v   v   con m   n   v   v   con   m   n   v   n
7. You decided to dip, but now you want to trip cause another brother noticed me.

art   m   n   pr art   n   v pr m   n   con   art   n   pr art
8. The newest version of the highway allows for more traffic; however, the benefits of the

n   pr n   v   v pr art n pr art   n
increase in traffic are offset by the cost of the project.

v n   v   m   m   m   n
9. Do you need more high speed data?

n con n v   con n v n v   m v   v n art m   m   n
10. Baby, if I knew what it was, I wouldn't have called it a "weird sparking thing."

PRACTICE FIVE

pr   n   n   v   v   m   n pr art n   con   n   pr art
1. In 1969, Celestial Seasonings began picking fresh herbs in the forests and canyons of the

n   con   v   n v   m   m   n
Rocky Mountains and blending them to create healthy, flavorful teas.

con m   m   n   v m m   m   m   n v m v   v   v
2. While fruit bearing trees are far more numerous, pine trees are older, having been growing

con   n   v   art n
when dinosaurs roamed the earth.

art   m   n   pr v   m   v   v   art m   n   m v
3. The greatest difficulty in fighting zombies is overcoming the natural desire not to hurt

m   n   con n m   v   con   n   v m   n
another human being, but you must remember that zombies are no longer human.

n   v m   v art m   n   pr art n   v   pr art   m
4. Nobody will ever deprive the American people of the right to vote except the American

n   n   con art m n con v   v n v pr m   v/n
people themselves, and the only way they could do this is by not voting.

n   v pr m   n   con n   pr   n
5. It smells like burnt baloney and regrets down here.

m   m   m   n   con n v   m pr n v con n   m   v   n   con
6. One very good reason that dogs are better than cats is that dogs actually do things that

116

```
     v    v    v   pr   m    n    con  n    pr   n
```
need to be done, like bomb sniffing and barking at strangers.
```
  int    m   n v   v    n      con n vm   v   n   v    v    n
```
7. Hey! Now we've got problems, and I don't think we can solve them.
```
     n   v   m    v   pr    n      v  art   m   n   con  n  v    v      n
```
8. You can always count on Americans to do the right thing -- after they've tried everything
```
  m
```
else.
```
   art    m   n   v    n    con  v    m   m        n       v  art  n  con
```
9. The first dogs were canids that lingered near human encampments, eating the trash that
```
    n    m   m   m    v    pr  m     n
```
people even back then produced in large quantities.
```
    m   n   pr art     m         n    v con  n  v   m  v    m  pr
```
10. One issue with the counseling department is that they are hard to get ahold of.

PRACTICE SIX
```
  con  pr art   n    pr m    n       pr art m   n   pr art    n     pr m
```
1. And for the support of this Declaration, with a firm reliance on the protection of Divine
```
    n      n    m     v   pr m    n  m  n   m    n     con  m   m     n
```
Providence, we mutually pledge to each other our Lives, our Fortunes, and our sacred Honor.
```
   m   n v m   n  n   v  pr art  n   pr m   n  con   v  pr art   n      v
```
2. Once it was my turn, I typed in the name of my topic and waited for the computer to give
```
 n  art    n
```
me the information.
```
   con  n  v   art    m    pr art  n  n  v   m  v  m     m   n   v   m   pr art
```
3. While I enjoy the portability of the iPad, it doesn't do enough real work to be useful in an
```
 m     n
```
office setting.
```
     n    v   n  v  n  con   n   v  art   m     m    m  n
```
4. Ma'am, can you tell us where you got the world's tiniest bow tie?
```
   con n   v  m   v      n  v   v  n m  pr art   n     art  n  pr m    n
```
5. If you are not delighted, we will make it right with a replacement or refund at your store.
```
     v    m   con   art   n pr   n    v   pr  n    v  pr   m      n      n v
```
6. To sum up, because the sink in question drains to pipes shared by multiple apartments, it is
```
    m     v    con art   n   v   m    m
```
impossible to state that "the tenant is clearly responsible."
```
  int   v n m  pr  v     n
```
7. Boy, am I sick of writing sentences.
```
    v     pr art  n  pr m    n  n n v m    n   n
```
8. Standing in the light of your halo, I got my angel now.
```
   art    m   m   n   v  art  n    v    v   m    n    m   n
```
9. The average wait time to see a counselor has been three weeks, every semester.
```
    art   m   n   pr   n      v   m  m   pr art  n   pr  m      n
```
10. The first settlers in New England were very aware of the effects of religious persecution
```
  con    n   v   v    v    n pr  n   con  n  m   v  n    v   con  n
```
because they had experienced it in England, but they still made laws dictating what people
```
   v    v
```
could believe.

ALL THE ANSWERS

PRACTICE SEVEN

   m   v   n pr art   n   pr   n   int
1. Never compare me to the mayor in *Jaws*! Never!

   n   v art n pr   n   v   v   con n   v   v   pr   m   m   n
2. There are a lot of ways to get killed, and she seems to stumble into every single one.

   n   v   n con n v   con   art   m   n   m   v m   pr   n   con
3. He informed me that it was because the other sinks involved were likely above mine, and
con   pr   n   m   n   v   v   pr con art   m   n   v   m
that due to gravity, my sink would back up while the higher sink would not.

    con n v   v   art m   n   n v   m   v   n   pr art n pr   n   con
4. When I am eating a new cookie, I am always paying attention to the level of sweetness and

   n   con m pr art   m   n
flavor and also to the cookie's softness.

   pr   n   v   art m   m   con   m   n   n v   v   v   m   m
5. In order to make a cheesy ham and potato casserole, you will need to gather together one
   n art   n   pr   m   n   m n pr   n   pr   n   n   con   m   n
onion, a package of frozen hash browns, one can of cream of chicken soup, and diced ham.

   art   m   n   v   n   pr   n v   n   con n   v   v   n   con
6. The best place to get donuts in Portland is Blue Ribbon, but you need to get there before
   n   v   m
they run out.

   int   int   n   m   v n v pr   n   con n v
7. Okay, okay, ladies, now let's get in formation cause I slay.

   pr art   n   art m   m n   pr m   n   con art m   m   n   v
8. In the restaurant, a grizzled old man with no teeth and a jaded young detective sat

    n/v art   m   n con art   m   n
discussing the murder case and the apple pie.

   n   v   m   pr n con n   v   v   n   v   n   v   con n v
9. Sonia felt terrible about it, but she had to hire someone to help her clean before she went
   m   m
completely insane.

   con n   v   m   m   n pr   n   n   v   v   n   m   n   con
10. If I were planning my last meal on earth, I would have fillet mignon, mashed potatoes, and
   m   m   n pr   n
eight different kinds of donuts.

CHAPTER 3

PRACTICE ONE
1. gerund
2. none
3. gerund
4. none
5.gerund

PRACTICE TWO
1. gerund
2. was turning--not a gerund

throwing a party-- gerund
3. gerund
4. none
5. gerund

PRACTICE THREE
1. none
2. none
3. none
4. gerund
5. gerund

PRACTICE FOUR
1. Working for the man--gerund
just trying to make a living--gerund
2. playing Monopoly--gerund
getting out of jail--gerund
3. gerund
4. gerund

ALL THE ANSWERS

5. gerund

PRACTICE FIVE

1. gerund
2. gerund
3. none
4. none
5. gerund

PRACTICE SIX

1. gerund
2. gerund
3. gerund
4. gerund
5. are showing-- none
   jumping-- gerund
   swimming--gerund

PRACTICE SEVEN

1. gerund
2. none
3. gerund
4. gerund
5. gerund

CHAPTER 4

Subject in bold and italics, predicate underlined.

1

1. **we** go independent

2. **I** want independent

where **classmates** are dependent

teacher is teaching independent

3. **They** are facing independent

they know independent

4. **we** missed independent

5. **You** wear independent

so that **nothing** will touch dependent

6. **I** can't get independent

7. **seat cushion** can be used independent

8. **those** discover independent

that **there** is dependent

9. **Carol Burnett** seemed to be having

independent

she gave independent

10. When **she** was dependent

she'd stop and lean independent

PRACTICE TWO

1. **I** have independent

2. **There** was independent

as **audience** waited dependent

what **she** would do dependent

3. **Getting** can be independent

when a **person** has lost dependent

4. do **we** have to get independent

5. As **preacher** speaks dependent

Sarah grips and bends independent

6. **I**'m watching independent

7. **You** can't handle independent

8. **I** have independent

that **children** will dependent

where **they** will not be judged dependent

9. **Jose** preferred independent

ALL THE ANSWERS

that **Yale** <u>made</u> dependent

10. **(understood you)** <u>Say</u> independent

PRACTICE THREE

1. **I** <u>consider</u> independent

2. **Thomas Merton** <u>wrote</u> independent

I <u>cannot discover</u> independent

if **I** <u>try to evade</u> independent

3. <u>can</u> **you** <u>see</u> independent

what **we** <u>hailed</u> dependent

4. **person** <u>needs</u> independent

5. **We** <u>are</u> independent

6. **(understood you)** <u>Watch</u> independent

7. **I**'m independent

I'm not going independent

8. **You** <u>can see</u> independent

when **team** <u>runs</u> dependent

9. no clause

10. **(understood you)** <u>Curse</u> independent

that **you** <u>put</u> dependent

PRACTICE FOUR

1. **We** <u>hold</u> independent

that **men** <u>are created</u> dependent

that **they** <u>are endowed</u> dependent

that **these** <u>are</u> dependent

2. **top** <u>is</u> independent

3. **undersigned**, <u>agrees</u> independent

4. **I** <u>hope</u> and <u>thank</u> independent

5. **I**'<u>ve</u> independent

(invisible that) **we**'<u>re</u> dependent

6. **I** <u>know</u> independent

that **this** <u>is</u> dependent

I <u>prefer</u> independent

where **I** <u>don't know</u> dependent

7. **You** <u>decided</u> independent

you <u>want</u> independent

cause **brother** <u>noticed</u> dependent

8. **version** <u>allows</u> independent

benefits <u>are offset</u> independent

9. <u>Do</u> **you** <u>need</u> independent

10. if **I** <u>knew</u> dependent

what **it** <u>was</u> dependent

I <u>wouldn't have called</u> independent

PRACTICE FIVE

1. **Celestial Seasonings** <u>began picking</u>

and <u>blending</u> independent

2. While **trees** <u>are</u> dependent

trees <u>are</u> independent

when **dinosaurs** <u>roamed</u> dependent

3. **difficulty** <u>is</u> independent

you <u>remember</u> independent

ALL THE ANSWERS chapter 4

that **zombies** <u>are</u> dependent

4. **Nobody** <u>will</u> <u>deprive</u> independent

way <u>is</u> independent

that **they** <u>could do</u> dependent

5. **It** <u>smells</u> independent

6. **reason** <u>is</u> independent

that **dogs** <u>are</u> dependent

that **dogs** <u>do</u> dependent

7. **we** <u>'ve got</u> independent

I <u>don't think</u> independent

(invisible that) **we** <u>can solve</u> dependent

8. **You** <u>can</u> <u>count</u> independent

after **they** <u>'ve tried</u> dependent

9. **dogs** <u>were</u> independent

that **people** <u>produced</u> dependent

10. **issue** <u>is</u> independent

that **they** <u>are</u> dependent

PRACTICE SIX

1. **we** <u>pledge</u> independent

2. Once **it** <u>was</u> dependent

I <u>typed</u> and <u>waited</u> independent

3. While **I** <u>enjoy</u> dependent

it <u>doesn't do</u> independent

4. <u>can</u> **you** <u>tell</u> independent

where **you** <u>got</u> dependent

5. If **you** <u>are</u> dependent

we <u>will make</u> independent

6. because **sink** <u>drains</u> dependent

it <u>is</u> independent

that **tenant** <u>is</u> dependent

7. <u>am</u> **I** independent

8. **I** <u>got</u> independent

9. **wait time** <u>has been</u> independent (Or the subject is only time)

10. **settlers** <u>were</u> <u>aware</u> independent

because **they** <u>had experienced</u> dependent

they <u>made</u> independent

what **people** <u>could believe</u>. dependent

PRACTICE SEVEN

1. **(understood you)** <u>compare</u> independent

2. **There** <u>are</u> independent

she <u>seems</u> independent

3. **He** <u>informed</u> independent

that **it** <u>was</u> dependent

because **sinks** <u>were</u> dependent

that **sink** <u>would back</u> dependent

while **sink** <u>would</u> dependent

4. When **I** <u>am</u> dependent

I <u>am paying</u> independent

5. *you* will need independent

6. *place* is independent

you need independent

before *they* run dependent

7. *(understood you)* let independent

cause *I* slay dependent clause

8. *man* and *detective* sat independent

9. *Sonia* felt independent

she had independent

before *she* went dependent

10. If *I* were planning dependent

I would have independent

CHAPTER 5

1

1. simple
2. compound/complex
3. compound
4. simple
5. complex
6. simple
7. simple
8. complex
9. compound
10. complex

PRACTICE TWO

1. simple
2. complex
3. complex
4. simple

ALL THE ANSWERS

5. complex
6. simple
7. simple
8. complex
9. complex
10. simple

PRACTICE THREE

1. simple
2. outside the quote marks=simple. Inside the quote marks=complex
3. complex
4. simple
5. simple
6. simple
7. compound
8.complex
9. Trick question! This is not really a sentence. It's an expression of emotion or an interjection.
10. complex

PRACTICE FOUR

1. complex.
2. simple
3. simple
4. simple
5. complex
6. compound/complex
7. compound/complex
8. compound
9. simple
10. complex

PRACTICE FIVE

1. simple

ALL THE ANSWERS

2. complex
3. compound/complex
4. compound/complex
5. simple
6. complex
7. compound/complex
8. complex
9. complex
10. complex

PRACTICE SIX

1. simple
2. complex
3. complex
4. complex
5. complex
6. complex
7. simple
8. simple
9. simple
10. compound/complex

PRACTICE SEVEN

1. simple
2. compound
3. compound/complex
4. complex
5. simple
6. compound-complex
7. complex
8. simple
9. compound/complex
10. complex

CHAPTER 6

1. none

2. compound subject
3. compound subject and compound predicate
4. compound sentence
5. compound predicate

1
values show in who that
complex sentence

national history, and the people
compound sentence

of animals while American
complex sentence

their artists, Chilean currency
complex sentence

face strange and might reject
compound predicate

2
Getting up in the morning has
gerund as subject

a night owl, but I do a few
compound sentence

time every day and always eat
compound predicate

It also helps if I start
complex sentence

When I can, my lovely
complex sentence

3.
of my house because I
complex sentence

annoys me and embarrasses
compound predicate

to do, I wouldn't have
complex sentence

my friends, but they live
compound sentence

my neighbors, but trusting them
compound sentence

4.
degree because of three false
complex sentence

comes from, but this is not
compound sentence

college is done while millions
complex sentence

are in school and should save
compound predicate

with debt, so students should
compound sentence

5.
an amazing shift because pets
complex sentence

it was hurt, and the police
compound sentence

communicate anything, and the
compound sentence

improperly, but the court
compound sentence

ALL THE ANSWERS

can communicate, certain
complex sentence

6.
really exist, but zombies are
compound sentence

a possibility because scientists
complex sentence

Nuclear weapons and killer
compound subject

ant's brain and controls
compound predicate

humans, a zombie outbreak
complex sentence

7.
from the ground, and
compound sentence

from the ceiling, the guano
complex sentence

falls to the ground and piles
compound predicate

the bats ate and pollens that
compound subject

the area, and those plants reveal
compound sentence

Chapter 7
1.
Every so often,
introductory element

fit anymore and

compound subject

old clothes when
complex sentence

different painting options,
compound sentence

On the other hand,
introductory element

2.
Lately,
introductory element

sleeping less and sleeping worse
compound predicate

different factors, one
complex sentence

wake up, the
complex sentence

To function,
introductory element

3.
people came out, he
complex sentence

Interestingly enough, he
introductory element

ten dollars while
complex sentence

with a credit card, but they
compound sentence

on their spending when

complex sentence

4.
gets a dog,
complex sentence

living a hundred years ago,
introductory element

in a sack and
compound predicate

care of that animal until
complex sentence

makes that commitment, a dog
complex sentence

5.
the morning, I
introductory element

day goes well and
compound predicate

contact lenses because
complex sentence

my dog going, I
introductory element

I eat breakfast, I
complex sentence

6.
video games, there
introductory element

game play, but
compound sentence

story, so you
compound sentence

the end or fight
compound predicate

human minds because
complex sentence

7.
of the world is
gerund as subject

fascinating and is
compound predicate

For example, the
introductory element

to the US because
complex sentence

In fact, there
introductory element

CHAPTER 8
1.
human noses, but
semicolon

For example, a dog
introductory element

or sorrow, different
complex sentence

skin, and they
compound sentence

However, the amount
introductory element

2.
zombie apocalypse, many
introductory element

unprepared and will
compound predicate

masks on because
complex sentence

wrong because
complex sentence

masks on zombies is
gerund as subject

3.
each year and
compound predicate

color of the leaves, it
complex sentence

exploration because
complex sentence

Unlike Columbus, Marco
introductory element

was basic, I
complex sentence

4.
of years, people
introductory element

gathered and went
compound predicate

a mammoth, they

complex sentence

in calories, so
compound sentence

starving, and eating
compound sentence

5.
pre-Roman times, people
introductory element

for the season, so
compound sentence

the streets, or
compound sentence

Interestingly enough, it
introductory element

religious, Christmas; and
semicolon

6.
Italian food, they
complex sentence

However, the
introductory element

with noodles and
compound predicate

to Italy where
complex sentence

they did because
complex sentence

7.

ALL THE ANSWERS

around them because
complex sentence

However, archeologists
introductory element

were lush and were
compound predicate

In fact, mammoth
introductory element

to insects so that
complex sentence

Chapter 9

1.
yoga regularly, and
compound sentence

anyone yoga, but
semicolon

at a desk, my
fragment

I can, I
fragment

yoga routine, but
compound sentence

2.
a wire filter, a French Press
fragment

beans and also more
compound subject

the coffee and traps them
compound predicate

strong coffee, and
compound sentence

does, or even worse
fragment

3.
exist there and ended
fragment

self taught and unable
compound predicate

communities, Chicago
fragment

Jazz era as rebellious
complex sentence

Beatniks, and the youth
compound sentence

4.
fascinating person, immensely
fragment

and pain, and she
compound sentence

her health, she
introductory element

brilliantly dark, and the
compound sentence

died young but
compound predicate

5.
fame which leads us

fragment

Worse than that, we
introductory element

picture, and no one
compound sentence

wealthy because they
fragment

Conversely, no one deserves
introductory element

6.
immigrant, and he
compound sentence

loved and valued the
compound predicate

optimistic, some people
complex sentence

approach, Capra Corn.
fragment

different, for he considered
compound sentence

7.
these days where
complex sentence

Darth Vader, dressing
fragment

kills people for no
fragment

emulating, a mass
semicolon

ALL THE ANSWERS

boring only because
fragment

Chapter 10
1.
were invented, they
complex sentence

a field, plowing
fragment

a purpose. Farmers
comma splice

had performed, but
compound sentence

forward; animals
run-on sentence

2.
However, there is
introductory element

States. That is the
comma splice

cookie, a vanilla cookie
sentence fragment

served warm when breaking
complex sentence

cold milk and shared
compound predicate

3.
England, they found
complex sentence

with elephants which
fragment

magical monsters, and the
comma splice

However, it is
introductory element

savages. In one battle
comma splice

4.
flooded, and silty water
comma splice

its banks, it left
complex sentence

Unfortunately, modern
introductory element

along, and the Nile
comma splice

international stature while
fragment

5.
the bank because
fragment

convenient; however, this
comma splice

creatures. Being alone
comma splice

the bank, but if people
compound sentence

people, the internet
complex sentence

6.
different jobs. It is
comma splice

badgers, and their legs
run-on sentence

badger burrow, the
complex sentence

for similar reasons, but they
compound sentence

race dachshunds because
complex sentence

7.
in history. That argument
comma splice

resources; before oil, people
run-on sentence

wealth, and all nations
compound sentence

example, they raided
fragment

soldiers, the reality
complex sentence

CHAPTER 11
1.
however, their
introductory element

there are drawbacks.

ALL THE ANSWERS

commonly misspelled word

delicious and are full
compound predicate

orange, their hands
commonly misspelled word

won't be too worried
commonly misspelled word

2.
dog person. That
Comma splice

like cats because
complex sentence

Whether you are
commonly misspelled word

swell shut and give
compound predicate

They're too cute
commonly misspelled word

3.
mainstream. Everyone
comma splice

There are two major
commonly misspelled words

PC games those
run-on sentence

online, like League of
fragment

other, but the important

compound sentence

4.
new apartment, there
introductory element

Will there be
commonly misspelled words

is good, it's
complex sentence

is bad, however,
complex sentence

it's like having
commonly misspelled words

5.
I get it; grammar
comma splice

are not your favorite
commonly misspelled words

writing, so I need to
compound sentence

professional life, writing
introductory element

moment comes, be
complex sentence

6.
for you because the news
fragment

However, the way people
introductory element

store once, and I overheard
compound sentence

very upset; she was
comma splice

sweetener, and she believed it.
compound sentence

7.
must climb because
complex sentence

at the base of the mountain
commonly misspelled words

climb with purpose.
commonly misspelled words

Check the weather
commonly misspelled words

or you're going to
commonly misspelled words

Chapter 12

1.
young people. Billions
question mark

their later years, most
complex sentence

of aging with creams
fragment

There is no
commonly misspelled word

why don't we?
direct question

ALL THE ANSWERS

2.
keep pets.
indirect question

needy, and Americans
comma splice

have pets, the answer
introductory element

is simple, the love
fragment

However, there are
introductory element

3.
No, it's a neurological
commonly misspelled words

many ways, through
semicolon

depression. They say
comma splice

to understand, and we all
comma splice

in their heads?
direct question

4.
Native Americans, the Cherokee
introductory elements

and books; there was
comma splice

However, white settlers

introductory element

resettlement treaty although
fragment

Is this fair?
direct question

5.
dog or a cat?
direct question

poops in your house?
direct question

trainable and able to
compound predicate

tricks like catching a Frisbee?
fragment

to ignore you?
direct question

6.
center and it's hard
commonly misspelled word

away as it is
complex sentence

an apple, but if a
compound sentence

a pie, the other
complex sentence

horrible because I
fragment

7.
our lives seems to
gerund

to do because the
fragment

Otherwise, we feel
introductory element

need the answer?
direct question

to ask the question?
direct question

Chapter 13

1.
dog person" or
quotation marks

cat person"?
quotation marks

of their identity.
commonly misspelled words

people say "I'm a cheese
quotation marks

a cotton person" with
quotation marks

don't matter, but there are
compound sentence

2.
ask if ... long?
indirect quotation

ALL THE ANSWERS

all year long.
indirect question

The barista said, "I don't know."
direct quotation

year round, it
complex sentence

special, and it is
compound sentence

3.
that said, "Goodbye... you."
direct quotation

I wrote back
new paragraph

learned that the ...cable.
indirect quotation

did die. That person
comma splice

heart attack, and EMT
compound sentence

4.
are small, they love to
complex sentence

people don't?"
quotation marks

with small children, it can
introductory elements

questions when they don't
fragment

conforming, so we need
compound sentence

5.
something is cool.
quotation marks

It used to be that other
complex sentence

which bad meant good.
quotation marks

people are; they want
comma splice

confuse the adults, and special
compound sentence

6.
yell, "Hey!"
direct quotation

me that he ... three blocks.
indirect quotation

hearing him; however,
comma splice

my own thoughts, I
complex sentence

street vendors, but I wish
compound sentence

7.
"No," she said.
Dialogue

"He can't come
Dialogue

come in. I am
Dialogue

not ready."
Dialogue

mother said that he
indirect quotation

she cried. "He deserves
Dialogue

Chapter 14

1.
whales travels thousands
Subject-verb agreement

every year in order to
semicolon

There are many
commonly misspelled words

characteristics, but linking
compound sentence

large bodies and provides
compound predicate

2.
our bodies is stress
subject-verb agreement

supposed to avoid stress?
direct question

flight situations, and we
compound sentence

ALL THE ANSWERS

 eieieieiechapter 14-15

tiger are not at
Subject-verb agreement

would pass because the
fragment

3.
that time, vinyl wasn't
introductory element

animal entrails.
indirect question

eat later, a process
fragment

the intestine was stretched
subject-verb agreement

drying rack when someone
complex sentence

4.
horses runs down
subject-verb agreement

a hill, and a bird twitters
comma splice

the sun call out
subject-verb agreement

invites you to hop
commonly misspelled words

It's always free
commonly misspelled words

5.
bad definitions. This leads
comma splice

What is the white
quotation marks

race? In reality
direct question

as a race. It is a
comma splice

history, were not
subject-verb agreement

6.
There are many
commonly misspelled words

America, there are
fragment

California, because they
complex sentence

sixty years, so a person
semicolon

other pet ... is not as good.
subject-verb agreement

7.
An alphabet.. was the first
subject-verb agreement

into clay and then dried.
compound predicate

parchment, specially prepared
fragment

Oftentimes, people
introductory element

sheep skin because the
complex sentence

Chapter 15
1.
my dog, a Wonder
semicolon

My niece loved it.
pronoun-antecedent

on her as soon
complex sentence

that my dog loved the gift.
indirect quotation

costume... taken it off.
pronoun-antecedent

2.
degrees which on camera
fragment

Sunlight... It is blue.
pronoun-antecedent

Actually, the color changes
introductory element

people can train themselves
pronoun-antecedent

these differences... to see them.
pronoun-antecedent

3.
people ... they begin to take
pronoun-antecedent

eieieieie131

ALL THE ANSWERS

adulthood, starting with
fragment

college or moving in to
compound predicate

apartments... are usually
subject-verb agreement

seems cool. To an adult,
comma splice

4.
industry ... the cars it produces
pronoun-antecedent

There is a chain
commonly misspelled words

one... is a copy of the Apple
subject-verb agreement

If China ... if it compensated
pronoun-antecedent

If China...it enjoys, is growth
pronoun-antecedent

5.
survive, especially in
fragment

People...they can find.
pronoun-antecedent

in brisk weather
commonly misspelled words

weather, but when it
compound sentence

A snow suit with... is
subject-verb agreement

6.
a woman applies for
subject-verb agreement

skills and far less likely
not a compound sentence

A woman... when she has
pronoun-antecedent

is not while people will
complex sentence

Consequently, men tend
introductory element

7.
humanity, they get
pronoun-antecedent

were able to identify
commonly misspelled words

mother, but we see
compound sentence

no father and is so
compound predicate

his fixation, he
introductory elements

Chapter 16

1.
popular when they first
complex sentence

Harry Potter and the Goblet of
Fire
title

carrying wands, and sales
compound sentence

Twilight and The Hunger Games
title

were also popular, they didn't
complex sentence

2.
poem "Stopping...Evening"
title

by Woods on a Snowy
title capitalization

one evening and ponders
compound predicate

of the year," he says.
quotation marks

possible in its current
commonly misspelled words

3.
is Orphan Black. It is
title

excellent acting though
complex sentence

like Sherlock and Top Gear
title

television show... that it feels

pronoun-antecedent

appetizers than a full meal.
commonly misspelled words

4.
is the <u>Mona Lisa</u>. It is
titles

There is a song
commonly misspelled words

called "Mona Lisa,"
titles

a poem called "Mona Lisa,"
titles

movie called <u>Mona Lisa Smiles</u>.
titles

5.
as Shakespeare. He was a
comma splice

<u>Doctor Faustus.</u>
title

"The Passionate Shepherd to His Love."
title

plays, <u>Henry VI</u>.
title

women and might have been
compound predicate

6.
called "Lose Yourself"
title

movie <u>Eight Mile</u>
title

He raps, "Man
quotation marks

This is true; food stamps
comma splice

the money for diapers?
direct question

7.
shows is <u>Supernatural.</u>
titles

It's in season
commonly misspelled words

from <u>The X-Files,</u>
titles

<u>Supernatural</u> is a fun
title

show, but it doesn't
compound sentence.

Chapter 17

1.
Tale of Two
commonly misspelled words

In <u>A Tale of Two Cities,</u>
titles

The cities' problems
possessive nouns

is corrupt while Paris
complex sentence

personal sacrifice; these
comma splice

2.
There is no
commonly misspelled words

my dog's snores.
possessive nouns

safe and content which
semicolon

snoring. It usually
comma splice

think that a person ...apnea.
indirect quotation

3.
is dense and filled with
not compound sentence

However, even academic
introductory element

authors...they don't
pronoun-antecedent

think, "I hope... understands me."
direct quotation

The author's ideas need
possessive noun

4.
waiting, and decided
compound predicate

ALL THE ANSWERS

The three birds' tails' feathers
possessive nouns

on fire, and they flew
compound sentence

The man's flame thrower
possessive noun

flame thrower... to have it
pronoun-antecedent

5.
A dog's eyes are
possessive nouns

a powerful thing, big and brown
fragment

up at me and starts making
compound predicate

Am I heartless?
direct question

a treat, she might have
fragment

6.
happened to Juan's
possessive noun

What happened to Juan's apples?
direct question

With Klaus's apples he
possessive noun

The children's apples were eaten
possessive noun

can, whether they were
commonly misspelled words

7.
There was a time
commonly misspelled words

the eagles' eggs
possessive noun

too thin
commonly misspelled word

nothing, but conservationists
compound sentence

feathers helped turn
gerund

Chapter 18

1.
the course of the war, Navies
introductory element

navies went from wooden
capitalization

war ships. There were even
comma splice

Ships moved south to
capitalization

the South while the first
fragment

2.
The winter is considered
capitalization

the Holiday Season but
quote marks

During the summer, we
introductory elements

have the Fourth of July.
capitalization

fireworks and hotdogs?
direct question

3.
Ohio; Chicago, Illinois;
semicolons

the city access
capitalization

The Missouri River was
capitalization

use freeways to do this
capitalization

same thing, but these old
compound sentence

4.
It's one of the strange
commonly misspelled words

the Empire State Building
capitalization

Many tall buildings...are topped
subject-verb agreement

benefits; they increase
comma splice

ALL THE ANSWERS

an international spitting
capitalization

5.
My brother met a
capitalization

monk and said
compound predicate

said, "How are you, Brother?"
direct quotation

gave my mom a jar of honey.
capitalization

walking around the garden.
capitalization

6.
The Vitamin String Quartet
capitalization

String Quartet is
subject-verb agreement

four musicians, usually
fragment

like "Don't Stop Believing" and
titles

It's very interesting to listen
commonly misspelled words

7.
creative costumes and eating
compound subject

more fun if they followed
complex sentence

Halloween's lead.
possessive noun

at Thanksgiving dinner
capitalization

If everyone... he or she would
pronoun-antecedent

Chapter 19
1.
thrift stores and finding
compound subject

cool, fashionable clothes
hyphen

to wear is a skill
commonly misspelled words

everyone has; some people
comma splice

My sister-in-law is one
hyphen

She is self-aware enough
hyphen

2.
cool people, people who
semicolon

person ... explodes behind her.
pronoun-antecedent

a devil-may-care attitude.
hyphen

Rumi wrote, "Sell your
135

direct quotation

bewildering, and that is
compound sentence

3.
an apple-pie-eating mood
hyphen

people... they will come up
pronoun antecedent

tremendous choice because
fragment

there are three kinds of
commonly misspelled words

The Dutch apple pie
capitalization

4.
that humankind has used
hyphen

service that dogs do, people
introductory element

dogs to the shelter and leave
compound predicate

them there. These people
comma splice

imagine a dog's inner life.
possessive noun

5.
a happy-go-lucky day?
hyphen

ALL THE ANSWERS

a get rich quick day
hyphen

or a garbage day?
direct question

friends days or dance
not compound sentence

dance-to-the-music-in-the-car
hyphen

6.
little Wonder Woman
hyphen

that my mom gave her.
capitalization

is too small for her
commonly misspelled words

a stupid-looking skirt.
hyphen

at night and is only able
compound predicate

7.
his life, and I want
compound sentence

Daniel's ex-boyfriend
hyphen

him baby's breath
possessive noun and hyphen

in a half-hearted attempt
hyphen

is only lukewarm?
direct question

Chapter 20

1.
Southern California which
fragment

is half great
hyphen

Two hundred days
numbers

and sunny, maybe more.
semicolon

with cancer, all of her
complex sentence

2.
There is a student
commonly misspelled word

borrowed $120,067
numbers

social work, a career
fragment

is $40,000 a year
numbers

massive loans to keep
fragment

3.
next to each other
Commonly misspelled word

If four farms grow

numbers

word problem, but I just
compound sentence

numbers, and there aren't
Commonly misspelled word

come up. Except in
fragment

4.
Eating out or eating... is
subject-verb agreement

home costs $4.50 in
numbers

in ingredients, but the same
compound sentence

2450 calories. That is
comma splice

will be 400 calories and
numbers

5.
It's not unique
commonly misspelled word

On the first day
numbers

After two or three days
numbers

the great sleep. That is when
hyphen

seven days, all of them

fragment

6.
the Founding Fathers began
Capitalization

in the 1700s,
numbers

However, the people in
Introductory element

a bad king, and now they
Comma splice

Now in 2018, many
numbers

7.
every year when people leave
complex sentence

called Black Friday.
capitalization

Do you need seven $5
number

human decency?
direct question

Then save all
commonly misspelled words

More information and the answers to the tests are available at madskillzacademics.com.

22500784R00077

Printed in Great Britain
by Amazon